The 9 Principles of Positivity

By Crystal Wolfe

Cover Design by Crystal Wolfe
Interior Design by Crystal Wolfe
Typography by Crystal Wolfe
Edited by Donald Hart and Crystal Wolfe

May 24th, 2024
FIRST EDITION

ISBN-13: 9781954258082

Library of Congress Control Number: 2024933625

PCCN: 9781954258082

A United World Press
New York, NY

7/13/24

Dear Jeeraine,

I hope you find this book uplifting!

[illegible]

Table of Contents

Dedication

This book is dedicated to everyone out there who has faced struggles, loss, trials, tests, tribulations, problems, failures, delays, and disappointments (i.e. just about everybody), and has never given up.

I hope this book helps you. I hope it will reach the lives of those who need it—to uplift, to inspire, to encourage, and to keep you going on this hard, beautiful, crazy journey we call life.

Thank you for allowing me the privilege to be a part of your journey, through this little book you hold in your hands. I am positive that we are all in this together, and together we can make a positive difference.

Together, we can turn our negative experiences into something good. Together, we can make this world a brighter place. One person at a time.

This book is dedicated to all of you.

INTRODUCTION

I wrote this book about "the principles of positivity" because I felt compelled to write something that would bring light, love, and inspiration to other's lives. Frankly I also wrote this book for myself—to try encourage, educate, and uplift myself!

Many people throughout my life have told me that I'm the most joyful and positive person they every knew, but I won't say that I'm always positive. I try to be. I am learning to choose to be.

I will guarantee you that there have been times when I was probably one of the most negative, unhappy, and miserable people you would never want to meet. I'm sure there are days to come that I won't be positive.

I'm human. And I'll never be perfect.

Yet I get back up, after my times of despair, (or just general irritability!)—I get back up and try again. That's the mark of a truly positive person—you never give up. You make mistakes, you fail, then you dust yourself off and keep right on going. I keep trying.

We all make mistakes, we all have failed, but it's how we react to the negative aspects of life that mark our character.

A positive person believes they're getting better as they go along. They believe that it's worth the effort.

Because it is. It really is.

In the course of my journey in life, I am now committed to being the most positive person I can be, as much of the time as I can be, while allowing for the imperfections and emotions that come naturally from lack of sleep, not feeling well, being overwhelmed, overworked, frustrated with trying to control the outcome, and just plain human.

None of us will ever be perfect this side of heaven. But I believe being positive is also about being real, and accepting people where they're at. In the dark times, the most positive thing we can do is just listen, care, and accept someone (or yourself) right where we/you're at.

It's okay to express our feelings. I validate that sometimes our problems can feel insurmountable. I don't want anyone to think this book is about ignoring problems, or discounting emotions.

I just want to encourage you to not give up in those tough times. To find and make something good from them.

The tough times grow and strengthen us. The hard things we go through can become lessons we learn that evolve us. The losses we face can make us more grateful for everything we have. When we make mistakes, we are humbled to know we aren't perfect, and that's a positive too. Humility is a good thing. It helps us to learn and grow.

Being mistreated helps us to become more compassionate to others, impassioned to fight for justice, and to help others who are mistreated. It teaches us to say no and to set healthy boundaries.

Enduring struggles makes us stronger. The problems we face help us to become more resourceful. When we work through them, we realize that every problem, big or small, really *does* have a solution.

Everything we've been through makes us who we are. If we do the work to not become bitter by the curve balls life throws our way, we can use those things to make us become better, stronger. Suddenly everything we go through becomes a blessing, something we can be grateful for.

Our mess becomes our message. Our tests become our testimony. Our lives become a legacy.

We all have a part to play. We were all born with a purpose. We are alive for a reason. We all have gifts, intelligence, and talents that the world needs. Writing this book is one of mine.

I'm setting my intention that this book will be the wind beneath your wings, a source of enlightenment on your own unique and wonderful path. No matter how small a part it plays, I hope that it touches your heart, opens and expands your mind, makes you smile, maybe even laugh a little at the occasional silliness, and feel seen, heard, respected, and loved. Most of all, I hope this book helps you to be more positive, (and I hope it helps *me* to be more positive too)!

I'm not an expert. I'm simply someone who truly cares. I see your value. I want to help you to see it too. Let's begin.

And coming to Him as to a living stone which has been rejected by people, but is choice and precious in the sight of God, you also, as living stones, are being built up as a spiritual house for a holy priesthood, to offer spiritual sacrifices that are acceptable to God through Jesus Christ. For this is contained in Scripture: "Behold, I am laying in Zion a choice stone, a precious cornerstone, and the one who believes in Him will not be put to shame." This precious value, then, is for you who believe; but for unbelievers, "A stone which the builders rejected, This became the chief cornerstone."

-1 Peter 2:4-8, NASB

The 9 Principles of Positivity

1. Positivity is About Choice
2. Positivity is About Emotion
3. Positivity is About Perspective
4. Positivity is About Gratitude
5. Positivity is About Openness
6. Positivity is About Focus
7. Positivity is About Growth
8. Positivity is About Action
9. Positivity is About Endurance

CHAPTER ONE
Positivity is About Choice

Ready? *Okay!* I hope most everyone knows that cheerleading reference. It's what cheerleaders often say when they begin their cheers.

So why did I begin with that? Because I want to be your cheerleader. I want to encourage you. I want to lift you up. I want us to turn our negatives into positives. I want us to take our power back. Together.

How? By recognizing that we have a choice in the matter. We have the choice to be positive—or negative. We have the choice to keep going or to give up. Everything in life is a choice. And everyday our choices—big and small—effect our future, and the lives of those around us.

Will we choose the path of least resistance, and go with the status quo? How will we react when things go wrong?

We can reflect and dwell on it. We can become easily angered and offended, but when we hold on to the negative things in life, those things become a poison that slowly kill us. Then that bad thing that happened hurts us over and over again, long after the incident that so hurt us. This is the definition of suffering.

I don't ever want to make anyone feel that their emotions aren't valid. I am so sorry for the things that happened in your life that gave you so much pain. I do want us—myself included—to work through our pain in a healthy way, so that it doesn't deter us from living our very best lives, as our very best selves.

We don't have to let our experiences hurt us over and over again. We don't have to let a trauma define us. We can process it so that we don't get blocked, stay stuck, and relive it over and over and over again.

I know this isn't easy. Still, how we react to the things that come our way is a choice. We can choose to ignore our problems and hope they just go away. I hate to break it to you—they won't.

So, what do we do? What's the positive way to deal with the curveballs that life throws our way?

We can accept our life as it is, while working towards where we want to go. We can face our problems—which takes courage. We can face ourselves—which takes even *more* courage. We can take responsibility for our part in our problems—that takes humility and maturity.

Instead of fighting life, we can learn to embrace it. Painful things are a part of life. Bad things happen to good people. And when good things happen to us, it's important to stay humble.

It's also important to remember that two wrongs don't make a right. If someone hurt you, I'm truly sorry, but please don't turn around and use that as a reason to treat someone else that way. They don't deserve any more than you did you. No one deserves to be mistreated.

We can tear down our own walls and defenses. We can become vulnerable enough to learn, to change, to grow, and that gives us strength. We can choose to do everything with sincerity and the right intentions. We can do our part, and trust and leave the rest up to a higher power.

How does that work? Examples are always a good thing. They tend to help us to understand concepts better.

Example: You just found out your spouse has cheated on you and wants a divorce. What is the most positive response? (This example is called diving right in to the deep end folks)!

Well, it's okay to feel the pain and grief and betrayal of what happened. Actually, you *need* to feel it to be healthy. It's a grieving process. You're mourning the loss of the person you expected to share your life with. You're mourning the loss of what you thought your life would be. And you're dealing with a very deep betrayal by what was likely one of the people you trusted most.

If you repress your emotions about it, it is likely to come out in your life in unhealthy ways. It's important to process what we go through in a healthy way.

Every person and situation is different. But there are standard ways to cope in healthy ways. There are also ways to cope in unhealthy ways.

Unhealthy Ways to Cope

1.) Cheating on your spouse the way they cheated on you.
2.) Getting into a new relationship and cheat on them the way your spouse cheated on you.
3.) Doing drugs
4.) Drinking too much
5.) Overeating
6.) Not eating enough
7.) Not sleeping enough
8.) Suicidal ideology
9.) Defeatist attitude

10.) Depression, anxiety, rage
11.) Engaging in promiscuous behavior
12.) Engaging in reckless behavior
13.) Entering into a new relationship before mourning the loss of your husband
14.) Getting into arguments and screaming matches with your ex
15.) Obsessing about your ex without a resolution
16.) Watching negative TV that makes you feel worse
17.) Engaging in social media hate campaigns
18.) Pushing your friends and family away and self-isolating
19.) Starting arguments with your friends, family, (even strangers) i.e. taking out your anger on those closest to you.
20.) "Kick the dog," so speak, i.e. bullying.
21.) Quitting your job (This is not a good time to make major life changes, unless you have good reason to leave and/or another job lined up)
22.) Moving without good reason
23.) Going on a shopping spree and spending all your money/savings on things that aren't worth it
24.) Listening to music that puts you in a funk and affects you negatively

Those were some unhealthy ways to cope. Now here are some healthy and positive ways of coping.

Healthy Ways to Cope

1.) Focusing on what you can do for yourself, i.e. self-care
2.) Exercising
3.) Praying
4.) Reading inspirational and positive spiritual books like the Bible and self-help books

5.) Learning a new skill such as French cooking
6.) Meditating
7.) Doing positive affirmations
8.) Listening to music that uplifts you
9.) Engaging in activities that bring you joy, such as dancing
10.) Going to church/mass/synagogue/etc.
11.) Engaging in positive activities with your friends, such as going to café together and having some coffee or tea
12.) Seeing a therapist
13.) Getting on medication to help you cope if needed
14.) Taking a vacation (it can be great to get a change of scene to clear your head)
15.) Watching positive TV to distract and uplift yourself (in healthy amounts)
16.) Watching positive videos on-line (but not too much, i.e. all day long)
17.) Calling a trusted friend, family member, or advisor to talk out your feelings
18.) Pet and play with your pet.
19.) Sitting with your feelings and trying to reframe your thoughts in a positive way (this is a hard one; however, it is important to deal with and process your emotions in the right place, way, and time)
20.) Working on your goals
21.) Doing nice things for yourself mindfully. It can be something as small as taking a bubble bath with bath salts and candles, or going to a spa and pampering yourself for the day
22.) Keeping a daily gratitude journal
23.) Joining a group: prayer group, Bible Study, support group, i.e. a positive group of some kind
24.) When and where appropriate, if you don't currently have a pet, adopting an animal. Taking care of, petting,

and cuddling with a pet can actually help with depression.

25.) Making a "To-Do List" and experiencing the infinite pleasure of crossing items off the list on a regular basis!

We cannot control so many things in life. We cannot control how people treat us. Inevitably, we will not always be treated right. But we *can* control who we allow into our lives. We cannot control a lot of our circumstances. But it is our decision how we *react* to them.

That is our choice. And our choices will absolutely affect the course of our lives.

We all get up and makes choices every single day. Will be do something positive and productive today, even on those days we feel tired, cranky, sad, etc.? Or will we stick with the status quo, doing just enough to get by?

Will we work towards our goals? Will we try to make life better? Or will we stay in bed watching bad movies and eating ice cream and cake? It's okay to have days like this every once in a while. We all need to veg and decompress. But when that becomes your lifestyle, you may have a problem!

What's an example of reframing your thoughts? Here's an inner dialogue for the example given above. Every situation and the people involved are always unique unto themselves, so please remember that these are just examples.

Reframed Thinking: *"I really loved my spouse. I am so grateful for the time we shared. I will always be grateful for those memories. I wish it didn't have to end, and I wish it didn't* *end the way it did, and I am trusting and believing that better things are in store for me.*

Everything happens for a reason. Even the worst things can be a good thing, if we do the positive work to make them so.

I hope that my spouse will be happy in their new life. I wish no harm to them and their new partner.

It may take work and time, but I believe I will also be happy in my new life eventually. I may be sad today, but that doesn't mean I will always feel this way.

I don't need anyone else to be happy. I am making myself happy. My cup is full cup and I am full of life. I am grateful for the journey and every experience, even this painful one. I will find the lesson in this, and I will become happier and find fulfillment—even if in this moment I am in incredible pain.

The pain will eventually lesson as I stay the course. I choose to forgive them. I choose to forgive myself. I do not condone their behavior and actions, but I radically accept that I cannot change the past, or anyone else's choices.

I am choosing to move forward. I am choosing life. I believe I have a bright future. I believe the best is yet to come."

I hope these examples helped you to see how working through the healing process can help ease the pain of what happened. You don't ever have to say that bad behavior is right. But if you don't forgive someone for hurting you, you're really just hurting yourself.

Let's say you're at a point when everything seems to be going wrong in life. Your dog dies. (No, this is not a country song!) Your house catches on fire and everything in it is destroyed. You get in a car accident and your car gets totaled. Someone close to you passes away.

You get the idea. If someone you loved is diagnosed with a terminal disease, of course that is not your fault. You deserve to be validated for that painful experience.

Maybe the car accident wasn't your fault, and maybe it was. Maybe you're the one who made the mistakes and are reaping the consequences, or maybe you are reaping the consequences of someone else's mistakes.

Choosing to blame yourself or others isn't going to help, however.

Most of us experience days and time periods like this. Especially if you're trying to live a spiritual life.

Being tested and going through trials is a way that the universe tests our character. It's a necessary part of the process to live your best life.

There are spiritual principles at play in all our lives. Certain tests are necessary to pass before we will have the qualities needed to achieve our own unique purpose for being alive.

One spiritual test is to continue to be grateful and praise God, even when everything is going wrong, like Job did. A part of trust is not having all the answers, but still choosing to trust that everything happens for a reason, even bad things can have a positive result, and every painful experience serves a higher purpose.

How do you know if you have a purpose? Well, you're breathing, aren't you?! The very fact that your alive means that you can be used to make a positive difference in this world. It is up to each one of us, every day of our lives, to choose whether or not we will make use of the opportunities afforded us.

We all have potential. We all receive opportunities. We can make opportunities for ourselves by going after what we want.

You have the choice to keep going after your dream job. Then at least you give yourself an opportunity for them to give the opportunity to you.

You lose 100% of the shots you don't take.

So, take a shot.

Expect to fail. Not every shot will go through the net. But you will start climbing the ladder of success because every door that opens is a shot you made. Every shot you don't make, provides lessons to help you receive even better opportunities—if you don't give up.

It is so empowering to recognize that we have a choice in who we let into our lives too. For so long I didn't realize that.

I thought that the people I was close to "chose me." I know I am not alone in this. A lot of people who have a pattern of being in toxic relationships don't realize they have a choice in the matter. But we do have a choice in who we allow into our lives—and who we don't.

Probably the single most positive thing I've done in my life, is cutting toxic people out of it. If we want to grow and flourish, we simply cannot do so while we're in the wrong relationships.

If you are in a relationship that is unhealthy in some way, or a relationship that is interfering with your goals and dreams, instead of helping you to achieve them, it may to time to end it. If you want to live your best life, these kinds of relationships probably can't continue.

People who are toxic can make us feel that we are dependent on them, and/or that they are dependent upon and cannot live without us. But just like at the end of the movie, "The Labyrinth" when Jennifer Connelly's character realizes the truth and speaks it: "You have no power over me," the house of cards that David Bowie's character carefully constructed comes tumbling down, to reveal that the power he pretended to hold over her was an illusion.

Many of us will have tests like this from the people in our lives. Tests that reveal our character and intentions. The hardest battle we will have to fight is the one that is within our own minds: our fears, our false beliefs, and our insecurities.

The reality is that it is more respectful to others, to help them to recognize their *choice* in every matter of their lives. It empowers us to recognize that our choices matter. They are important.

It is empowering to see the part we play in the outcomes. When we make mistakes, as we all do, we can choose to allow ourselves to become sad, frustrated and discouraged. We can look at our lives and become overcome by regret so that we cannot do anything.

Or we can accept that's what's done is done. It is what is, and choose to learn from it. Choose to make the best of it. Choose to do it better next time. Make better choices next time. Make better use of the opportunities that come. Avoid the pitfalls where and when we can. Believe that you *can* have better, that you *will* have better, that you *deserve* what you want, and then *work* for it.

Our choices affect our lives. Absolutely. They also affect the lives of those around us. And in intricate ways we will never know, our choices have an effect on the world.

Positive choices and decisions will eventually lead to positive results. Even before our good actions pay off, we can enjoy the journey a lot more when we're making healthier choices. It makes for a much better ride!

Choosing to be positive also takes discipline. It takes discipline and persistence to make consistently good choices. To exercise and eat healthy on a regular basis, is a choice, for example, that will help your muscles *and* your mind stay strong.

Experts say exercising regularly decreases the chances of ALL types of diseases across the board by 80%.

Our bodies were made to move every day. Our body needs fruits, vegetables, and protein to stay healthy. This also helps us to make better decisions because our minds are clear. Excessive alcohol and sugar may contribute to brain fog and digestion issues.

We cannot control the outcome. As we make positive and healthier choices, our lives will begin to reflect that. We will enjoy the journey a whole lot more along the way.

Seeing positivity as a choice doesn't mean ignoring your problems or pain. It is acknowledging that pain, validating it, but rather than giving into it, choosing to not let it define you, or control and dominate your thinking and actions on a permanent basis.

Seeing positivity as a choice, takes away the victim mentality and turns you into a winner, simply by your self-will to not let anything—or anyone—keep you down. It is also positive to work through and process the negative things you've been through.

It is not being positive to pretend that problems don't exist. Rather, it exhibits positivity to face them, do something about them, and not allow your problems, past, or circumstances to control you in the present, and destroy your future.

You are not your past. What happened to you is not who you are. Rather, it helped to make you who you are: and that's a *good* thing! You can use all the negative experiences to make you stronger, kinder, more compassionate, and more resilient.

But that is your choice.

We all make these choices every day.

What will your choice be?

PRACTICAL APPLICATION
For Positive Choices

Prayer

Dear God, I pray that your will be done on earth as it is in heaven. I pray that your will be done in my life. Please help me to recognize the choices in my life, and choose to make the best choices for myself, and for all involved.

Please give me the strength and discernment to make wise choices. Please enable me to consider the good of all involved when I make my choices. Please help me to make positive choices that positively affect everyone. Amen.

Meditation: Meditate 5 minutes today on a good choice you've made in your life and the wonderful things that have happened as a result of that positive choices.

Then meditate 5 minutes on a time you made the wrong choice, the consequences you incurred for it, and how you did better next time, or can do better in the future.

We don't learn without making mistakes, so it can be a good thing to make mistakes. Instead of feeling bad about them, find the positive in them, and do better next time!

Affirmations

I choose to be positive today.

I choose to believe that whatever negative feeling or circumstance I am going through will pass.

I choose to believe that the best is yet to come.

I choose to believe I can have what I want.

I choose to believe that everything happens for a reason.

I choose to believe that I have a purpose.

I choose to believe I am right where I need to be.

I choose to believe that the right people and opportunities will come into my life at the best time.

I choose to be positive today—right now!

Declarations

I praise you because I am fearfully and wonderfully made; I know your works are wonderful. (Adapted from Psalms 139:14)

I trust in the Lord with all my heart and soul. I do not depend upon my own understanding. In all my ways I submit to Him, and He makes my paths straight. (Adapted from Proverbs 3:5-6)

I will not overcome evil with evil, I will overcome evil with good. (Adapted from Romans 12:21)

Song

"I Hope You Dance"
By LeeAnn Womack

I hope you never lose your sense of wonder
You get your fill to eat but always keep that hunger
May you never take one single breath for granted
God forbid love ever leave you empty-handed

I hope you still feel small when you stand beside the ocean
Whenever one door closes I hope one more opens

Promise me that you'll give faith a fighting chance
And when you get the choice to sit it out or dance

I hope you dance
I hope you dance

I hope you never fear those mountains in the distance
Never settle for the path of least resistance
Livin' might mean takin' chances, but they're worth takin'
Lovin' might be a mistake, but it's worth makin'

Don't let some Hellbent heart leave you bitter
When you come close to sellin' out, reconsider
Give the heavens above more than just a passing glance
And when you get the choice to sit it out or dance

I hope you dance
(Time is a wheel in constant motion always rolling us along)
I hope you dance

I hope you dance
(Tell me who wants to look back on their years and wonder)
I hope you dance
(Where those years have gone?)

I hope you still feel small when you stand beside the ocean
Whenever one door closes I hope one more opens
Promise me that you'll give faith a fighting chance
And when you get the choice to sit it out or dance

Dance

I hope you dance
I hope you dance
(Time is a wheel in constant motion always rolling us along)
I hope you dance
(Tell me who wants to look back on their years and wonder?)

CHAPTER TWO
Positivity is About Emotion

Let's talk about something hard. Something controversial. Something many people don't like as much…and then let's turn it positive.

Emotions. Feelings. Being vulnerable. Some people aren't comfortable with this, but these tend to be those who do not know how to utilize their emotions to make them work for them.

Emotions are not good or bad—positive or negative—without intention and actions making them so.

Emotions can fuel us. Emotions are the gasoline in our car. We can't go anywhere without them. They're our foundation. They're a critical aspect of being human.

Personally, I also feel comforted in the company of emotional people. The truth is, lack of human emotion is a red flag.

It's okay to feel. It's *good* to feel. It's necessary for your success and growth to work through and process your feelings so that you can learn how to use them for your good.

Psychiatrists want to give you medicine to repress or control your emotions. Doctors want to diagnose it. Those on social media want to judge it. The world at large seems to look down at our displays of emotion…*and yet?*

And yet our feelings are what make us human! Our emotions show that we care. Our vulnerability opens us up to love. And even when love ends in heartbreak, isn't it always better to have loved and lost, than never to have loved at all?

Isn't the ability to connect to someone deeply, one of the most beautiful gifts in life? When someone shows you that they care, isn't that the best thing they could do to help and uplift you? Doesn't it make you feel better, when you know that someone understands and cares about you, and what you're going through? Doesn't empathy comfort you to receive, and isn't it an honor to show compassion and empathy to others?

No emotion is negative. All emotions can be used for good, and for positive action.

It is a process to work through the pain and grief you might feel if things didn't end as you hoped. If you experienced betrayal in a relationship, or mistreatment, at first you may feel bitter, angry, and resentful. That is natural. Those wonderful emotions are teaching you that you deserve better and you will no longer tolerate that behavior. They are teaching you to love yourself.

Painful emotions are a part of life. Avoiding them leads to suffering. Pushing them away doesn't work. When you try to suppress your painful emotions it's like trying to hold a volleyball underwater. You won't be able to hold them down forever, and when they do come up, they will come up with a vengeance that is more likely to be destructive.

The way to process our emotions is to work *through* them. Allow yourself to *feel* them, but don't hold on to them. Let them go. It is a delicate balance.

Another powerful emotional tool, though incredibly difficult to cultivate for most people, is radical acceptance: "It is what it is." We cannot change the past. And if we want a better future, we need to accept what's done is done—in the present.

I'm not saying it's easy. I'm saying it's important to move forward in order to have a better life.

You can HAVE emotions, but don't have to let them HAVE you. You are NOT your feelings. You HAVE feelings.

You are not your thoughts,
you are not
your emotions.
You are
the "I" underneath,
you are your soul.

-www.abby-wynne.com-

Feelings are apt to change and come and go. But when you find the strength to CHOOSE to be positive no matter how you FEEL that's when you'll begin develop your character, and take control over your emotions, and your LIFE.

Even the most difficult relationships often have a lot of good things in them as well, that made you want to enter into that relationship to begin with. If you allow yourself to feel the pain, the anger, the sadness, even the rage, and do things to work through it, then you can eventually look back at the good parts of the relationship and appreciate them. You'll be able to look back at the good times and not be bitter that they ended. You'll use that relationship as a lesson that taught you something and made you better, got you that much closer to the love you really desire and deserve.

Being positive isn't about ignoring emotions, pushing them down, repressing them, or pretending like you don't even have them. Being positive is about working through them.

No emotion is good or bad, that our actions don't make it so. That means that anger, sadness, resentment, exhaustion, frustration, can be used for good, even for the positive. Let's explore this deeper.

Anger lets us know that something is wrong in our lives. There's something we're allowing into our lives that isn't right. It could be how we're being treated at work or in a relationship. Maybe it's time for a change. Maybe it's time to defend ourselves. Maybe it's time to move on.

Yes, being pleasant and polite, having respect and manners is a wonderful thing. But at some point, when you're not being treated with the respect you deserve, it's okay to have boundaries, it's okay to say no, and it's okay to say your peace.

I can't tell you when it's time to speak up. There are times to "kill people with kindness," and there are times to say, "How you're treating me is not okay," and then take action. Discerning what to do in any given situation takes soul searching, reflection, and discernment. Ultimately, you've got to do what you feel is right in the moment.

However, remember this: nothing, and no one, is worth your peace of mind.

Being sad is the other side of the coin of anger. They say depression is anger turned inwards. Anger and sadness are positive in the sense that they are like a light, like a beacon, shining a spotlight on what's wrong in our lives. That can be a good thing if we work on improving and changing what doesn't make us happy, isn't good for us, and to do more of what we love.

Being emotionally mature doesn't mean shying away from your problems. It doesn't mean shying away from discussing difficult topics. People who emotionally mature are comfortable navigating through the complexities of life and relationships, and aren't afraid to apologize when they're wrong too.

It's not just about being able to define and explain and express feelings and emotions openly, but also about handling conflicts and disagreements in a healthy way.

You can handle anything life throws your way. You got this.

Starting a disagreement with a positive, without blame or criticism, can make a big difference in how the conflict gets resolved. According to a study by psychologist John Gottman, 96% of the time, the way a discussion starts determines how it will end.

If you want your relationship conflicts to get resolved in a relatively healthy and constructive manner, having the emotional maturity to begin the conversation gently, rather than with anger, contempt, or criticism, will usually make all the difference not just in the discussion, or this relationship, but in your *life.*

We can learn new and better ways to communicate with others. Yet miscommunication is a natural part of life too. Unfortunately, I believe that misunderstandings are the number one relationship killer.

Keeping the lines of communication open is really important. So is taking into consideration other people's learning styles, personalities, and love languages.

We also have to work on how we think about and talk about and to ourselves. If we're down on ourselves, that's going to bring down our emotions. Some healthy ways to regulate your emotions can be found in the list below.

Healthy Ways to Regulate Emotions

1.) Getting balanced sleep is imperative to help with brain fog and emotional regulation. Keeping to a consistent sleep schedule is important to maintaining good sleep. People can vary, but the average amount of sleep need to have an optimal day is 7-8 hours of sleep.
2.) Getting regular exercise is important to mental and emotional health. Our bodies were made to move. It used to be that doctors said people needed at least 2.5 hours of exercise a week. Current research says it's better to get 5-7 hours of exercise a week.

3.) Having a balanced diet can prevent a lot of diseases, help your mind stay clear and alert, help you to feel rested when you sleep, and help to stabilize your emotions. All food is comprised of different properties that help your body in different ways. Blueberries and walnuts, for example can help to regulate your mood. Carrots contain Vitamin A that are good for the eyes. You are what you eat. So having a healthy diet can help you to stay healthier holistically.
4.) Treating physical illness is important. Getting your teeth cleaned twice a year, brushing regularly, and flossing daily will help to prevent cavities and even strokes, for example. It's important to take the medication for our bodies and our minds as prescribed.
5.) Avoiding mood-altering substances, such as excessive alcohol and drug use can help to maintain a balanced state. For example, smokers think smoking can help them to sleep, but it is actually a stimulate. Wine may help you to get to sleep faster, but you may not get as restful of a night's sleep.
6.) Taking a healthy number of vitamins and supplements can help your body to get what it needs that you may not be getting from your diet.

We have to radically accept the things we can't change—such as other people—and make peace with it. There are some things we won't be able to change. Others things we can only try to change, with no control over the outcome.

Controlling people often feel out-of-control. They think if they can control others, and their circumstances, they'll find stability. But that's a false sense of stability. We all have to work out to find the inner strength and resolve to be stable from within—apart from anyone in our lives—regardless of what is happening in our lives.

In reality, God is in control. Everyone is on their own journey. If we want to evolve, we need to respect where others are at, and focus on our own growth and actions.

It's more positive to focus on solving your own problems than to try to fix someone else's. It more positive to work on the issues in your own life than to try to control others and tell them what to do.

It is empowering to take ownership of our actions. By taking responsibility for the problems in our lives, we can learn the lessons of how to overcome them. If we continue to blame others for our lot in life, we will not live our best life. If we want a better life, then we've got take responsibility for it.

Regardless of the result, our efforts matter. We can all do our part. Then we can surrender and accept the outcome. We can find peace in knowing we did our best to foster a positive outcome.

If your job is doing what you love, you will never work a day in your life. That's what we should be working towards. Creating a life for ourselves that's doing what we love to do, will fill us with joy and energize us every day to do what's on our schedule.

It may take time, for living the life of your dreams rarely happens overnight.

For example, to make a living from my book sales, I've had to work multiple jobs as I'm working to procure enough events year-round to sell my books. Sometimes we might have to have a side hustle as we work towards living our dreams.

But if we face our problems head on, eventually things will work out. Things will get better a little more every day. Then, even when we aren't there yet, when we don't have *everything* we want, we can be positive and grateful for how far we have come, and confident of where we are going.

When we have a proven record of success in meeting smaller goals, and take small steps forward every day, that can aid us on our journey. If we keep doing so, eventually we will end up where we want to be. It helps us emotionally to feel a sense of accomplishment by achieving small goals.

On the other hand, if we cheat to get ahead, taking the easy way out of our problems, and into the position we want, we probably won't have the chops to do the job, and we won't have the mental fortitude to handle it as well as would have if we'd earned it. In the modern work place this happens a lot, but earning your way to the top, or wherever you want to be, is a much greater victory!

You are likely to feel more secure that you'll stay where you're at, when you've earned it. When you've built yourself, and your life up, brick-by-brick, you will probably feel more self-assured that it cannot so easily be destroyed.

Even if it is destroyed, you'll know you have what it takes to build your life from the ground up again! And again. And again. If that's what it takes. For as long as it takes to get it right.

It's natural to be emotional when times get hard, when things go wrong, when you expected something good to happen, and something bad happens. Whatever and however you feel about it is okay. The key is to let yourself feel it, then work through it to process it in a healthy way.

Then it becomes a lesson. Then it will make you better. Then you be stronger because of it than you were before.

The most important thing, is to not let your feelings stop you from whatever you believe you are meant to do.

Example: You go into business with your best friend. Five years go by and your business becomes successful. Then your best friend and business partner becomes greedy and finds a way to betray and cut you out of the business that you started together.

That sends your life on a downward spiral. You pretty much lose everything as a result—your car, your home, your fat bank account.

Is any of that your fault? No. Did you cause it? No. Yet there's still a lesson in it. Yet it still can be used to make you grow.

It would not be human to not be upset about all that loss and betrayal. So, what do you choose to do about this injustice? Everything in life comes down to our choices.

Some people use alcohol, drugs, or a fast and furious lifestyle to cope. I have compassion and understanding for that. But ultimately it is a way to avoid and escape your problems.

Working through our problems allows for the tears. Exercise helps us to release the anger and tension in the body. There is a lot of toxicity in our world today. This toxicity can get trapped in the body.

Movement, and any type of exercise really, helps to release any trauma and toxicity trapped in the body. Therapy can help to give you more healthy coping skills and tools to get through the tough times.

I encourage you to allow yourself to sit with the anger. Feel the sadness. Feel the loss. Then once you have felt it, and accepted it, you can begin again.

On the plus side, you know you can build a successful business. You know you have what it takes. You can think about having contracts to safeguard and protect yourself from this happening again.

What is not healthy is to suspect that everyone will throw you under the bus like that friend did.

Everyone is different. There are trustworthy and good people in the world who will help you, not harm you. It's important not to judge every other person in the light of one person you trusted who betrayed you.

When we get betrayed, if we work through it, we can still live a productive, positive and happy life full of good relationships. We can still live our best life. We can always go forward. Every day is a chance to make life better, even if it's just a little better than the day before.

You may decide to start a new business on your own. You may want to work for someone else for a while. You may write a book to help you release your thoughts and feelings about what happened. Writing and journaling is a wonderful way to cope and work through your feelings.

You may join a band and write music, or have some kind of creative outlet that turns this negative thing that happened into something positive that can help and uplift others as well as yourself.

Do not fear your emotions.

It is okay to be angry, but not to act out in violence. It is okay to get sad sometimes, but not to come to the point where you no longer want to live.

If you take your anger and turn it into a nonprofit that fights for justice, that's amazing. If you take your sadness, and use it to make enlightening works of art, that's a beautiful thing.

Your emotions can fuel you, energize you, give you purpose, and direction. Many people do not know how to handle other people's—or their own—emotions. Sadly, many of us were never taught the positive side of our feelings, or the best ways to cope with them.

We can teach ourselves as adults what we may not have learned growing up.

Have faith that you are strong enough to face your problems and work through your emotions on your own. It's a blessing to have emotional or any kind of support. Be sure to appreciate it if you do. However, if you don't, you still have what it takes to live your best life. You can still heal, and grow, and become better, all on your own.

When we exercise, and build our muscles, we become stronger and healthier for it. Ultimately it is up to us to become healthy and fit. No one can exercise and eat right for us. No one can take over own responsibilities for us. No one can go to therapy for us to learn healthy coping skills, and learn how to heal our own wounds. These are all components of having a healthy mental and emotional state that we must choose to do for ourselves.

Humans need to move. In the modern day, when so much of our lives revolves around sitting and computers, phones, gaming, and many other types of technology, many people are not making time for movement and exercise. Yet this is such a critical way to release and work through our emotions.

The emotions can get stuck in different parts of our body. When we exercise, these emotions are released in a healthy way.

Exercise is a positive tool to work through our emotions. "You are what you eat," is also a part of having a healthy mind, heart, and body. Taking the time to prepare our own meals and have a balanced diet is a way to stay healthy and prevent a lot of diseases. It aids us on being, and staying, positive. It is an important component of working through our emotions in a positive way.

In many ways, our emotions are the core, or the seat, and the foundation of our lives—of our success—or failure.

If we find we aren't able to regulate our own emotions, it's okay to seek help with the aid doctors and medication. It is positive to seek and find the help you need and deserve.

This world can get rough, and you are not weak to get help. You are stronger and better off in looking for aid. Getting help when you need it is an act of bravery and courage.

We can harness our anger, like a purifying fire. We can utilize our tears to act as a healing catharsis. We can use our humor to laugh at our cares, which makes our problems seem smaller and more manageable. Humor and laugher can be as healing as our tears.

We can choose to enjoy our life, no matter how difficult the situations we find ourselves in. We can learn to use our feelings for positive things and the greater good, and to manifest exactly what we want.

For those of you, that like me, have strong emotions, let's learn to funnel them into achieving exactly what we want. If you dream it, you can achieve it. Our dreams are meant to come true.

Thinking positive helps to make us feel better. Our emotions govern our thoughts, our thoughts lead to action, and our action leads to positive outcomes. Our minds, actions, and emotions have a big impact on results.

While we cannot control the outcome, or anyone in our lives, we can work on the discipline of our actions, mind, and utilizing our emotions for good. We can learn to control ourselves, and become less reactive.

We can make a positive impact by using our emotions to show compassion and empathy for others. The world is starved for kindness. It really uplifts others when you show that you care for them.

Leave playing games for the basketball court or the football field. Don't play with other people's hearts—or you may eventually get played. You will eventually reap the seeds you sow.

Being honest and open with your feelings, and allowing yourself to be vulnerable, is an important step towards intimacy in relationships. Don't allow anyone to play with your head or emotions because that isn't healthy for you. That's not love. That's not friendship.

Become the person you hope to find. Give what you would like to have. Treat people like you would like to be treated. Help whomever you can, whenever you can.

Then look for people who have compassion and empathy for you because that fosters a healthy, reciprocal relationship. Look for people who are rooting for you, are happy for you when something good happens, and help you when they can and you are struggling. That isn't easy to find. But it is worth the wait.

You have the right to protect yourself. When you tolerate toxic behavior with people who have no interest in changing or bettering themselves or their lives, it's going to be a major, if not insurmountable block to fostering positivity in your own life.

To be a positive person, you can't tolerate negative people and situations. To a certain extent, we all have to deal with these situations. We all have work through our own negative behaviors and beliefs too.

But we can choose who we allow into our lives. We can choose to find another job, if the job we have now is detrimental to us in some way. We deserve to have respect in our lives. Nothing—no job or relationship is worth your peace of mind. And if you don't have peace of mind, your emotions are going to become unstable and chaotic. Because there's no real positive, healthy way to have a toxic person in your life. Their toxicity will act as a poison.

All human life has value. And it is healthy to forgive everyone everything they do that hurts us. But forgiveness does not have to mean reconciliation. If there's been no change, and they are unwilling to change, then they will most likely just keep hurting you. Loving someone does not have to mean being close to them.

This is a decision we all have to make for ourselves in our relationships and in our lives. If you're not happy with something in your life—working to change it will help you to become a happier and more positive person, who feels positive and stable *most* of the time.

PRACTICAL APPLICATION
For Positive Emotions

Prayer

Dear Lord, please help me to see what my emotions are telling me today. If I'm frustrated and feeling overwhelmed, perhaps I need to rest, so that I can tackle things from a place of strength and peace.

Please help me to listen to my emotions, mind, and body. Please help me to learn how to use my emotions for good. Amen.

Meditation: Meditate for 5 minutes today on what you're feeling. Any feeling, whether it's painful or pleasant. Focus on the feelings that arise in you, allow yourself to feel it/them, validate it/them, accept it/them, then release it/them. Ask the universe to help you let your emotion(s) go so that it/they no longer cause you harm.

For another 5 minutes, focus on the light. Bask in the presence of a brilliant white golden light shining down on you. Lift up those emotions and watch them getting fused into the light. Then feel that beautiful warm light surround, embrace, and encompass you, lifting yourself up as you become the light, full of bliss and positivity.

Affirmations

I am safe to express my feelings.

I am working through my emotions in a healthy way.

I am lovable even when I feel emotional.

I will not take other people's emotions personally.

I choose to see the humanity in emotions.

I am using my emotions as a guide to show me where I need to work on myself and my life.

My feelings are not who I am—they're where I'm at and what I'm feeling right now.

I accept how I feel right now, and work through and process my feelings in a healthy way.

I accept that it is natural to have emotions, and I will not allow my emotions to *have* me.

Declarations

I refuse to be anxious about anything. In everything I do, by prayer and supplication, and with thanksgiving I let my requests be made known to God. And the peace of God, which surpasses all my understanding, guards my heart and my mind in Christ Jesus. (Adapted from Philippians 4:6-7)

In my anger, I refuse to sin. I will not let the sun go down on my anger. I will not give the devil a foothold in my life. (Adapted from Ephesians 4:26-27)

As God's chosen child, holy and dearly loved, I clothe myself with compassion, kindness, humility, gentleness, patience and love. (Adapted from Colossians 3:12)

Song

"You'll Never Walk Alone"

Original showtune by Rodgers and Hammerstein
From the 1945 musical "Carousal"

When you walk through a storm
Hold your head up high
And don't be afraid of the dark
At the end of the storm
There's a golden sky
And the sweet silver song of the lark

Walk on, through the wind
Walk on, through the rain
Though your dreams be tossed and blown
Walk on, walk on, with hope in your heart
And you'll never walk alone
You'll never walk alone

When you walk through a storm
Hold your head up high
And don't be afraid of the dark
At the end of the storm
There's a golden sky
And the sweet silver song of the lark

Walk on, through the wind
Walk on, through the rain
Though your dreams be tossed and blown
Walk on, walk on, with hope in your heart
And you'll never walk alone
You'll never walk alone

CHAPTER THREE
Positivity is About Perspective

What is a positive attitude or perspective? Well, a part of it is *expecting* things to work out. And while you're working towards what you want, developing patience in the process. Developing trust to believe that good things are on the horizon, even if you don't see it quite yet.

Even while we wait, we can be positive and happy. Even when it takes more work and time before things come together. We know that before the end things will work out. So, if they haven't worked out YET, then it's not OVER yet!

We can choose to be joyful. We can choose to be grateful. We can choose to look for ways to be uplifting to others. We can choose to have a good attitude. We can choose to look at our lives from a higher perspective.

One thing we can do to encourage others, is give a compliment a day, or better yet, try to find a sincere compliment or encouragement to everyone you meet every day of your life.

I started doing this as a child, when my grandmother told me how her father's philosophy was to give a compliment a day. I immediately adopted that philosophy for myself.

Then I thought, why not compliment everyone I meet? Then I thought, why not just offer any sincere compliment I see, given the appropriate person, time and place?

If someone is feeling down, they may need more encouragement than one kind word. So, my philosophy is to not withhold voicing the good things I see in others because it usually uplifts and validates people to have the good qualities they have acknowledged.

A good attitude is also about treating people the way we want to be treated. It's giving to others what we want for ourselves.

It's being patient and waiting with a hopeful attitude in the "mean" time. It is not easy to wait. It is not easy for most of us, but being patient while you work hard towards your goals is imperative to your success. Being patient means having a good attitude while you wait.

Some of us have had so many bad things happen to us that we literally become afraid to have hope. I've been there. But we all *need* hope. That's a very important part of life. Hope is like sunshine, and we all need a good dose of Vitamin D every day to stay happy and strong.

If you don't have hope, no wonder you feel depressed and like what's the use? But guess what? At any point in your life, you *can* turn your life around. And you *will,* with the right attitude!

There is always hope.

It may be hard to believe that sometimes. It may be hard to feel it sometimes. And it is the truth even so.

If you think it might help, you could make a list of goals and then map out practical, small steps you can take to achieve them on a daily, or at least on a regular basis. Then as you accomplish each small step, reward yourself with a little something special.

Take the time to celebrate your successes and accomplishments. Celebrate when you solve a problem, or reach a goal. It could be a nice meal, a beautiful new outfit, a coffee at Starbuck's or your local café. Celebrate your victories, great and small, even if it's a party of one! Part of *enjoying* life is *celebrating* life.

On the other side of having a defeatist attitude, is having a work-a-holic attitude. I've been there too. The extremes are not healthy. Do your best to strike a balance.

I definitely work hard, but I enjoy myself as well. I'm trying to enjoy the things I need to do on a regular basis that helps my mental health, such as exercising. I enjoy nature, so whatever the season, I try to get out in it and enjoy its beauty—the constant changing and shifting of the trees, the leaves, and the light.

We all need to clean ourselves every day, right? Why not do it with "mindfulness?" Mindfulness means maintaining a moment-by-moment awareness of our thoughts, feelings, bodily sensations, and surrounding environment through a gentle, nurturing lens. It means being in, and focusing on, the moment.

Why not set an intention that when you take a shower, or a long, luxurious bubble bath, that this is something nice you're doing for yourself? It's something that will soothe your muscles, relax your nerves, and calm your mind. You're doing something to take care of yourself. By doing it with mindfulness, you will enjoy it even more.

Something as simple as lighting a candle can be a celebration of life, or a way to create serenity in your living or work space. Believe it or not, by practicing mindfulness during self-care, eventually you raise your self-esteem and experience more self-respect.

Another good attitude to have, is to see everything as an opportunity. Let's say you go to an audition or a job interview and totally mess it up. What's a positive perspective you could have about it?

Well, there's always next time, right? What did you learn from it? What can you take from it that will make you better on the next go around?

Specifically, how would you dress different? Would you change anything about your demeanor? A good demeanor would be to have confidence, but not arrogance.

Were you prepared? How would you prepare better next time?

There are other jobs and other opportunities that will come your way with the right attitude. The right attitude wins friends and opportunities. And it helps you to go through life with a positive perspective that makes life more enjoyable for yourself, and for everyone around you.

Ways to Have a Positive Attitude

- Cultivate optimism. Believe that things will get better.
- Surround yourself with positive people. That will help you to stay focused on the positive. We become like the company we keep.
- Try not to focus on things that you have no control over.
- Maturity is being able to be happy even when you don't get what you want. Accept that not everything will go your way.
- Don't give in to the negativity even in difficult situations. Believe that every problem has a solution and there is always hope.

- Strive to improve your life and the lives of those around you. Even though you can't control the outcome of your efforts, try to find joy, peace, and comfort, in the effort itself.
- Use challenging situations as an opportunity to grow or learn. Have the courage to face and work on your problems.
- In spite of everything you have gone through, or are currently going through, do not allow it to make you a lesser person, instead help it make you a better, more compassionate person, who practices kindness, compassion, and empathy towards others.

At the end of the day, you're always going to be with yourself. Isn't it more fun to look at life as an endless opportunity to get it right, and to celebrate it when you do?

Doesn't it feel good to have hope? Doesn't it feel good to believe everything will work out—to have faith? Doesn't it feel great to have a good attitude and believe that life will deliver all your hopes and dreams, so long as you work hard, pass your tests, and never give up?

This book you're holding in your hands is one of my dreams come true. If God helped me to achieve this dream, He will help me to achieve more dreams. If God did it for me, He can do it for you!

Every step along the way I need to pause, take a moment, and be thankful, enjoy it, appreciate it, and always remember the hardships I endured and the sacrifices I made to be where I am. I'll tell you what, all the heartaches I've been through make the victories that much sweeter!

I believe in my dreams. I believe in your dreams too. I believe that all of us have hopes, dreams, callings, and goals for a reason. It will make the whole world a better place if I fulfill my purpose. It will make the whole world a better place, if you fulfill your purpose too.

Living your purpose will change your life. It will positively influence the lives of those around you, if you live your dreams. You will live your best life, when you begin to believe you CAN have what you want, you deserve it, and act AS IF you already have it.

As you begin to live your dreams, and you see all your hard work paying off, in other words, after you get to the other side, everything you went through to get there will be like another you in another life.

I'm getting there. I want to get there. I want you to get there and be there with me. I hope that you get there. And I hope that this dream that came true that you're holding in your hands will have some small part in your eventual, *inevitable* success.

Every cloud has a silver lining. Rain makes the flowers grow, and it makes the grass greener. Good can be found in anything. There's a lesson in everything.

There is a positive and a negative side to any situation. It's all about perspective. We get to choose our perspective, and which side we're on.

We may not realize we have a choice because it has become a habit to focus on the negative. A pessimist can become an optimist, if they choose to change their thinking.

We can all do this. It takes work. It takes practice. It takes discipline. And it takes time. But choosing to be more positive in life will change our perspective of life so that we enjoy it so much more. As will anyone around us!

Our mindset doesn't just make a difference, it makes ALL the difference! I can do it. I *will* do it. Doesn't that *feel* better than saying things like:

1.) Nothing ever works out for me.
2.) Things always go wrong in my life.
3.) It's always three steps forward and two steps back.
4.) No one cares about me.
5.) I'm never picked for things.
6.) Nobody likes me.
7.) I am so alone.
8.) Nobody cares.
9.) I'm never going to succeed.

Now let's turn these statements around with the positive version of them:

1.) Things are always working out for me.
2.) Everything always turns out right.
3.) I'm making progress every day.
4.) I'm grateful for those who care about me. I care about others.
5.) It feels good to be chosen for things and recognized for my talents and skills.
6.) People like me—and I like people! I'm a people person.
7.) I am never alone.
8.) I care.
9.) I will succeed—as long as I never give up!

You can see that how we think directly affects how we feel, what we do, and our future.

FYI, unless it's for the positive, never and always are generally words to stay away from. Even if you have some kind of bad habit like smoking, you're not *always* smoking, for example.

In relationships it's not accurate or fair to say, "You NEVER support me." Or "You ALWAYS let me down." Saying things like this discourages the other person from the very thing you want from them.

A better way to handle your disappointment is to limit what you're talking about to an isolated incident. You may use other examples, but try to always start with at least one a positive when you want to confront someone about something.

It's better to say, "I really appreciate how you take the trash out every Friday night. I'm often tired after a long work week, and it gets cold in the winter and hot in the summer so I really appreciate you doing that. Thank you."

Then: "I hope you don't mind if I mention something that has been on my mind lately. Even though I want to make sure you know how much I appreciate the hard work you do around the house, it would really mean so much to me if you could help out with X, Y, and Z. It would make me feel supported and loved. What do you think? Is this doable with your schedule and everything you've got going on too?"

I can't guarantee what their answer will be. But coming at them like this, I would like to believe in a healthy relationship they will at least try to do the things that will make you feel happy, supported, and loved in your relationship. At least compromise with you, by doing X and Y, even if they can't do Z right now.

Isn't so amazing how we can turn our whole lives around, simply by how we look at it? Our perspective. Our mindset. Our thinking. It can literally change the whole course of our lives. It can literally change how we look at our lives *right now.*

"As a man thinketh in his heart so he is." That's Proverbs 23:7, and it's also the name of an excellent little book about positive thinking by James Allen, *As a Man Thinketh.*

The battlefield of the mind is the greatest, hardest, most challenging battle most of us will ever face. Once you've conquered that battle going on in your own mind, it's a lot easier to face anything negative that life throws your way.

Life isn't easy. And there are so many blessings along the way that we can enjoy, if we choose to have a positive perspective in the midst of the storm. When you're able to maintain a positive attitude, regardless of the problems in your life, and *enjoy* life, even *with* your problems, then you have really become strong in who you are, and have grown so much.

Remember: life is not just about the destination. It's about the journey. Even when you do everything right, sometimes things will still go wrong. So don't be too hard on yourself. Self-talk makes a difference too. Don't be surprised if how you talk about yourself reflects in the people around you and how they treat you.

People treat you how you allow them to treat you. If you want to be treated with respect, respect yourself. If you want to be loved, learn what it means to love yourself first. If you can learn to be happy on your own, then anyone who comes into your life will be icing on the cake.

When it comes to perspective, think of an eagle. From our standpoint down on earth, our problems can seem so big. But from a higher perspective, our problems lose their power over us, because we know there is a reason and a lesson behind every problem. We know that every problem has a solution, and if we keep trying, we will find it.

As we mature, when something "bad" happens, we may ask ourselves, "What can I learn from this?" And "What is this experience trying to teach me or reveal to me?"

Even if you didn't do anything to cause it, even if it isn't your fault, what can you take responsibility for, that will help to prevent you from another negative experience similar to it next time, or make things better? It could also be about cultivating patience. For example, if you pray to God to develop the quality of patience, more than likely different difficult scenarios will arise to test your patience.

There could be something great waiting for you on the next horizon, if you keep going.

As you learn the lessons of life, and develop positive qualities like patience in the midst of the trial, you will grow, and higher lessons will come, and soon enough, before you know it, you'll realize you're at the mountain peak. You've been climbing for a long time, one step at a time, one lesson at a time.

From the vantage point at the top of the mountain, all of those hard things you went through made you stronger. And all of it, even the worst of it, is beautiful. Because all those moments make up your life. They make up who you are. And you are magnificent.

PRACTICAL APPLICATION
For Positive Perspective

Prayer

Please God, help me to see my life through your eyes, from a higher perspective. Help me to have right thinking. Help me to know the truth and embrace it. Reveal what I'm not seeing that will bring me clarity and direction. Help to recognize my value, in you, apart from everyone and everything else.

Please dear Lord, help me to have the right attitude today. Help me to have the right attitude in the circumstances I find myself in. Help me to be patient, and understand that anything good takes time. Help me to wait for the *right* opportunities. Help me to make the most out of every opportunity.

Help me to see the good in every circumstance, or at least find something that I can learn from it. Help me to keep the faith, and rise again, no matter how many times I get knocked down. Help me to never give up, and know that things will get better, in Jesus' name. Amen.

Meditation: Meditate 10 minutes today on something that happened in the past. And instead of feeling sadness, regret, anger, or anything else along those lines, reframe it.

What good came out of it? What did you learn from it? And remember, that what you went through then helped make you the great person you are today—one step closer to living your best life.

Affirmations

I accept where I am at.

I am enjoying working towards my goals.

I am making progress each and every day.

I believe that I deserve good things in my life.

I choose to see the positive in this situation.

I can do anything I set my mind to.

I believe that every cloud has a silver lining.

I can overcome anything.

I believe that everything is working out for me.

I can change my life, simply by changing my perspective.

Declarations

I will not be conformed to this world. I will be transformed by the renewal of my mind, and by this test I will discern what is the will of God, what is good and acceptable and perfect. (Adapted from Romans 12:2)

My light and momentary struggles are helping me to achieve an eternal glory that far outweighs them all. I fix my eyes not on what is seen, but on what is unseen because what is seen is temporary, and that which is unseen is eternal. (Adapted from 2 Corinthians 4:17-18)

I would have despaired, had I not believed that I would see the goodness of the Lord in the land of the living. I will wait for and hope for the Lord with a stout heart. I will patiently wait for and expect the Lord to come through, with confidence and faith. (Adapted from Psalm 27:13-14)

Song

"While I'm Waiting"

By John Waller

I'm waiting, I'm waiting on You Lord
And I am hopeful, I'm waiting on You Lord
Though it is painful, but patiently I will wait

And I will move ahead bold and confident

Taking every step in obedience

While I'm waiting I will serve You
While I'm waiting I will worship
While I'm waiting I will not faint
I'll be running the race even while I wait

I'm waiting, I'm waiting on You Lord
And I am peaceful, I'm waiting on You Lord
Though it's not easy no, but faithfully I will wait
Yes, I will wait

And I will move ahead bold and confident
Taking every step in obedience

While I'm waiting I will serve You
While I'm waiting I will worship
While I'm waiting I will not faint
I'll be running the race even while I wait

I will move ahead bold and confident
I'll be taking every step in obedience, yeah

While I'm waiting I will serve You
While I'm waiting I will worship
While I'm waiting I will not faint

And I will serve You while I'm waiting
I will worship while I'm waiting
I will serve You while I'm waiting
I will worship while I'm waiting
I will serve You while I'm waiting
I will worship while I'm waiting on You Lord

I will serve You while I'm waiting
I will worship while I'm waiting
I will serve You while I'm waiting
I will worship while I'm waiting

CHAPTER FOUR
Positivity is About Gratitude

Being grateful in every circumstance is spiritual maturity. By recognizing and appreciating what you have, the universe will give you more. But your intention behind what you say or do is essential to the best possible outcome. Our intentions behind what we do are more important than what we say or do.

Everything we do should be done with love, and love begins with sincerity. Being frustrated because you don't have what you want, and have worked hard for, is understandable. We've all been there. It's okay to vent, or jump and down, cry it out or whatever. Take all the time you need.

After you get it out, hopefully you can dig deep to find a few things grateful for. Because being grateful makes whatever you have more than enough.

It takes humility, and maturity, to recognize that no one owes us anything. We don't inherently deserve everything we want. We've got to earn it.

Then when we do, we will be even more grateful for it. We will appreciate it more. We will take better care of it. And because of all those things, we will be less likely to lose it.

We can set our goals and intentions, and as we work towards them, gratitude helps us to enjoy the journey more. Gratitude reminds us to slow down, take stock, and celebrate all the victories along the way.

Most people don't get everything they want in an instant. And unfortunately, those who do often lose it all quickly because they don't know how to be good stewards of it.

It is better to earn what you get through good, honest work and developing your God-given talent(s) and intelligence. Then every victory along the mountain you're climbing you will have earned.

Joyce Meyer says, "Complain and remain, or praise and be raised." If you complain along your journey, you will be walking around the same part of the mountain for a very long time.

Believe me, I've been there. I've been around that mountain countless times, and I suspect there are days ahead that I'll go around it once more. Most of us will have to pay our dues—and that's a good thing.

Even though I know I have many days, when I'm like, "ARE WE THERE YET??"

That's okay. No one is perfect. We all have off days. And days we just need to peace out and take a break.

Some days it's just better to stay in bed and veg. That's okay. Resting and expressing our thoughts and feelings can be helpful to work through them too. Give yourself a break every once in a while, and you will be so much better off for it.

Breaking a habit takes time. So does making a habit. More than likely, we will backslide, and that's okay—as long as we get right back up on that horse and try again. THAT'S what makes a winner.

Winners never fail because winners never quit.

Finding the good in the bad is a big part of being a winner. And the power of positive thinking can alter the trajectory of your life.

Winston Churchill said, "A pessimist sees the difficulty in every situation; an optimist sees the opportunity in every victory."

We can *expect* setbacks, disappointments, delays, and many nos and rejections on the journey of life. We can expect life to bring us challenges and pain. It's how we handle them that signifies if we are learning the principles of positivity. And it's how we handle them that builds—and reveals—our character.

There's just something about gratitude that unlocks blessings. It takes down roadblocks. It makes a way for miracles.

There's something about being thankful that makes God smile. Something about having faith even when everything is going wrong, that pleases the Lord.

That "overnight success" is often years in the making. Most people don't know what it takes to be successful, until they've put in the work.

Of course, all of this is easier said than done, but the goal is to learn to be happy even when we don't get what we want, even when we aren't successful, even when everything seems to be going wrong. That's a big part of being spiritually mature—being grateful and positive for your life even while dealing with your problems.

When you're able to find something to be grateful about in the problem itself, that a good sign you're really growing. Being grateful helps us to enjoy every moment of life—not just the good ones, but the hard times too. It truly promotes joy.

Gratitude is a principle of positivity because it's able to turn the darkness into light in a matter of moments. When you start thinking about all you have to be grateful for, it really feels good.

Chase those positive thoughts and feelings. Seek things to be grateful for, and I know you will live a much happier life, even if you face more challenges than most. Remember: the greater the dream, the more challenges you are likely to be required to overcome, to attain it.

10 Ways to Become More Grateful
By Robert Emmons

1.) **Keep a Gratitude Journal.** Establish a daily practice in which you remind yourself of the gifts, grace, benefits, and good things you enjoy. Setting aside time on a daily basis to recall moments of gratitude associated with ordinary events, your personal attributes, or valued people in your life gives you the potential to interweave a sustainable life theme of gratefulness.

2.) **Remember the Bad.** To be grateful in your current state, it is helpful to remember the hard times that you once experienced. When you remember how difficult life used to be and how far you have come, you set up an explicit contrast in your mind, and this contrast is fertile ground for gratefulness.

3.) **Ask Yourself Three Questions.** Utilize the meditation technique known as Naikan, which involves reflecting on three questions: "What have I received from __?", "What have I given to __?", and "What troubles and difficulty have I caused?"

4.) **Learn Prayers of Gratitude.** In many spiritual traditions, prayers of gratitude are considered to be the most powerful form of prayer, because through these prayers people recognize the ultimate source of all they are and all they will ever be. What if we didn't take good things for granted? Learn how gratitude can lead to a better life—and a better world.

5.) **Come to Your Senses.** Through our senses—the ability to touch, see, smell, taste, and hear—we gain an appreciation of what it means to be human and of what an incredible miracle it is to be alive. Seen through the lens of gratitude, the human body is not only a miraculous construction, but also a gift.

6.) **Use Visual Reminders.** Because the two primary obstacles to gratefulness are forgetfulness and a lack of mindful awareness, visual reminders can serve as cues to trigger thoughts of gratitude. Often times, the best visual reminders are other people.

7.) **Make a Vow to Practice Gratitude.** Research shows that making an oath to perform a behavior increases the likelihood that the action will be executed. Therefore, write your own gratitude vow, which could be as simple as "I vow to count my blessings each day," and post it somewhere where you will be reminded of it every day.

8.) **Watch your Language.** Grateful people have a particular linguistic style that uses the language of gifts, givers, blessings, blessed, fortune, fortunate, and abundance. In gratitude, you should not focus on how inherently good you are, but rather on the inherently good things that others have done on your behalf.

9.) **Go Through the Motions.** If you go through grateful motions, the emotion of gratitude should be triggered. Grateful motions include smiling, saying thank you, and writing letters of gratitude.

10.) **Think Outside the Box.** If you want to make the most out of opportunities to flex your gratitude muscles, you must creatively look for new situations and circumstances in which to feel grateful.

The goal is to find happiness and be positive, regardless of the outcome. Then nothing and no one can rock you off course. And if you stay the course, I have total faith that you will achieve wonderful and rewarding things in your life, that add to your happiness, and those around you as well.

Gratitude has the effect of helping us to refocus on positive emotions. It guides us to take an optimistic, solution-oriented approach to the challenges that we encounter in life. Both of which are hugely important to building resilience. Resilience, in turn, improves our overall quality of life by enabling us to bounce back from the hardships we will inevitably face at different points in our lives.

Gratitude is a positive way for people to appreciate what they have, instead of always reaching for something new in the hope it will make them happier, or thinking they can't feel satisfied until every physical and material need is met. Gratitude helps people to refocus on what they have, rather than on what they don't have.

Another way we can express our gratitude, and promote healthy, long-term relationships is by appreciating the good in the people in our lives. We can do this with our words, with a thank you note, with a gesture of goodwill, a gift, or a basket of muffins, or a tray of cookies.

Gratitude shows us that we wouldn't have all the good things we've been blessed with, without the help of others. By showing those in our lives that we appreciate them, it will connect us, and hopefully uplift and encourage them. It helps us to become more kind by telling others the ways they've helped us by being in our lives.

This helps us to foster and grow more positive, loving relationships. Just as you would like to be appreciated for your hard work and the good things you do, it's important to show our respect and appreciation for others.

It edifies them. And it elevates us.

The following are some known benefits of practicing gratitude:

- Being grateful can help us work through our trauma.
- Grateful people make healthier choices, like exercising regularly.
- Being grateful raises self-esteem.
- Being grateful improves mental health.
- Practicing gratitude promotes better sleep.
- Being grateful to others fosters stronger social bonds.
- Being grateful is a boost to our immune system and our heart health.

- Being grateful can helps us to calm down and improves our nervous system.
- Being grateful helps us to have better communication.
- Being grateful deepens and builds our resilience.
- Practicing being grateful will strengthen your ability to have positive recall in dark times.

Choosing to count your blessings every day and be grateful, turns you into an optimist, and what's wrong with that? It feels good to believe that everything will work out. It makes going through the hard times a lot better and easier.

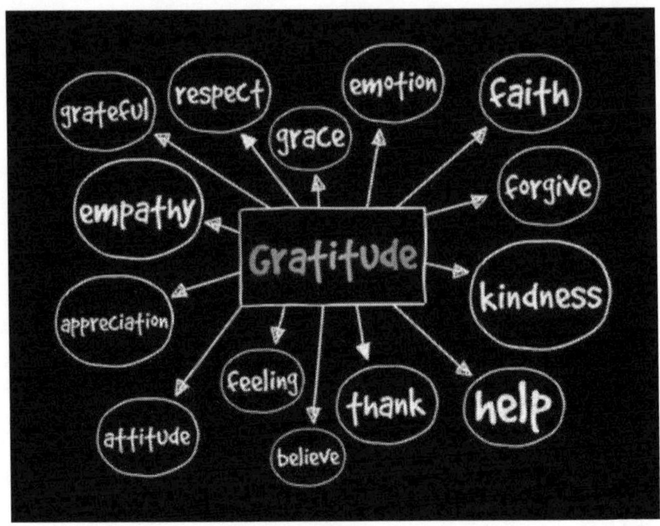

Taking pleasure in the simple things can really make life the day-to-day grind more enjoyable. Simple things, such as spending the day with a dear friend, eating a delicious meal you really had a taste for, or taking a walk and watching the beautiful colors of the sky as the sun goes down, can become so much more special and meaningful, if we would only take the time to truly appreciate them.

There will never be another day like this one. There will never be another sunset like the one tonight. Will you look out your window, or be out amongst the sky? Will you appreciate the sunshine of the day?

Will you stare out at the stars tonight, and remember when you were little, and wished upon a star? Can you remember how you felt then, how you truly believed that your wish would come true, with the pure, simple faith of a child?

True love is real and it exists. And dreams really do come true.

Remember that .you, that *you* before the world broke you down, who truly *believed* that everything was bound to work out, and try to believe that way again. Because while it's important to emotionally and spiritually mature, it's also beautiful to retain that childlike awe and wonder of this wonderful world we live in, with the simple and powerful faith that if God told you that something was going to happen—IT WILL—NO BUTS.

Gratitude probably won't make your problems go away, but you'll be able to cope with them a lot better. It will also help you to have a bigger support system when you really need it. And if you continue to work on solving your problems, eventually you will.

At the very least, if you're able to make peace with your problem, then in a spiritual sense, you made friends with it. In a similar way, when you pray for your enemies, you make friends of your enemies.

By choosing to be grateful, you can literally change your life, turn your negative experience into something positive, and turn your challenges into an adventure.

If you choose to be grateful, no matter what painful circumstances you find yourself in, eventually the universe will give you something to be grateful about! Of course, the same goes for complaining, but would you rather look on the dark side, or the bright side?

Let's look on the bright side and count our blessings. Then we will watch them grow, day-by-day, and one-by-one, until suddenly we realize we're happy with our lives, even *before* we get everything we want.

We can do this. By being grateful for what we have.

PRACTICAL APPLICATION
For Positive Gratitude

Prayer

Thank you, God for all you have given me. I am so grateful to have you in my life. I am so grateful for my blessings. I am so grateful for my salvation. I am so grateful for the air that I breath. I am so grateful for this gift of life you have given me. I hope to use it for your glory, for the good of others and myself.

Thank you for my clothes, and for food and water to drink. Thank you for the simple, little things that I don't want to take for granted when millions of people don't have their own transportation, a roof over their heads, heat, enough food to eat, and running water.

Thank you for the big things, like every goal I achieve that gets me one step closer to living the purpose you placed on my heart. Thank you for growing me, showing me where I need to change, and helping me to do it. Amen.

Meditation: Meditate 10 minutes today on something you prayed for that has come to pass. Meditate on the gratitude you feel about that answered prayer. Relish in the feelings that are evoked by achieving that goal or dream.

Additional Practical Step: Make a list of all your blessings. If you do this every day, you will see a positive difference in your attitude, and in your life. This will help you to start looking for the positive, looking for things to be grateful for, and in turn you will begin to recognize that your life is a gift.

Affirmations

I am grateful for everyone in my life. Even difficult people help me to grow.

I am grateful for everything I have.

I am grateful for my suffering because it brings me closer to God and makes me a better person.

I am grateful for my difficult circumstances because it helps me to learn.

I am grateful for the good things in my life.

I am grateful for God's unconditional love.

I am grateful for everyone who loves me, and who I love. I am grateful to share love.

I am grateful to have another day to get things right.

I choose to be grateful today—right here and now!

Declarations

Whatever I do, in word and deed, I do everything in the name of the Lord Jesus, giving thanks to God the Father through Him. (Adapted from Colossians 3:17)

I am always rejoicing. I am praying without ceasing, and I give thanks in all circumstances, for I know this is God's will. (Adapted from 1 Thessalonians 5:16-18)

Bless the LORD, O my soul.
I will remember all His blessings.
He has forgiven all my sins,
healed all my diseases.
He redeems my life from the pit.
He crowns me with steadfast love and mercy,
and satisfies me with good
so that my youth is renewed like the eagle's.
(Adapted from Psalm 103:2-5)

Song

"What a Wonderful World"
By Louis Armstrong

I see trees of green, red roses too

I see them bloom for me and you
And I think to myself
What a wonderful world.

I see skies of blue and clouds of white
The bright blessed days, the dark sacred nights
And I think to myself
What a wonderful world.

The colors of the rainbow
So pretty in the sky
Are also on the faces
Of people going by
I see friends shaking hands, saying, "How do you do?"
They're really saying, "I love you."

I hear babies cry, I watch them grow
They'll learn much more
Than I'll ever know
And I think to myself
What a wonderful world
Yes, I think to myself
What a wonderful world.

CHAPTER FIVE
Positivity is About Openness

An open mind is not usually encouraged in this day and age. And yet it is so critical for effective leadership and a healthy outlook on life. Being open is an important principle of positivity.

Unfortunately, many of us have lost the ability to respect others who hold different values and opinions than our own. The truth is, all of us deserve respect. You and your ideas deserve as much respect as anyone else's.

If you want to receive respect, isn't it fair to show respect to others? Isn't it right to treat others how we would like to be treated?

In many ways, being open to people and ideas is just getting back to the basics of humanity.

Often, nowadays, if someone is of a different political affiliation, and says something we don't agree with, we cut them off and out of our lives. Is this how happy, healthy, well-adjusted individuals respond to differences?

No one is going to agree with what you think and say and do 100% of the time. That's a fact. It's natural. And it's okay to have disagreements, and your own opinion. Just as it's okay for someone else to have their own opinion.

The reality is that even if someone shares your religion and political party affiliation, they are still going to disagree with you on some things. They will have their own preferences on food. They may not share the same hair color or way of dressing and speaking.

While it's not necessary to be friends with everyone, it is important to be able to listen and engage others in conversation who have vastly different views than you do, with an open mind. This is a very important aspect of learning and growing.

Openness is also important in fostering positive change in your closest relationships, and for better communication skills. By agreeing to disagree in your love relationships, finding a middle ground and compromise that both of you can agree with, your relationship will continue to blossom and grow by showing each other respect.

In politics, it's important to try to respect everyone's perspective and views. One, you can learn from people who think differently than you do. Two, to make positive change on a mass level, it's best for both parties to come together and find a solution that's win-win. Or at that very least, that both parties feel they have gained something.

Personal problems don't get solved when it's "my way or the highway." Most people won't respond positively to that kind of attitude.

Important issues don't get solved when both political parties stubbornly refuse to back down or compromise. So many people are suffering as a result of people individually, and as a whole, not coming together, for the greater good.

There's a Garth Brooks country song called, "Burning Bridges," with lyrics that say, "Like ashes on the water, I drift away in sorrow, knowing that the day my lessons finally learned, I'll be standing at a river, staring out across tomorrow, and the bridge I'll need to get there, will be a bridge that I have burned."

Consider the image below. Carefully consider the meaning behind it.

I hope and pray that person dangling in the middle of that bridge won't ever be you or me. And I hope we can learn to build bridges, instead of tearing them down. I hope we can learn to respect other people's interests and beliefs, and not tear people down either.

Everyone is coming from different backgrounds, cultures, and has different knowledge than we have. If we remain open, we can learn valuable lessons from others that we might not have learned otherwise. The same way others can learn from us, our knowledge and expertise.

May I ask—are you a person who's always looking to make their next point in a conversation? Because having two ears and one mouth means that we are meant to listen twice as much as we speak. James 1:19

states that we should be quick to listen and slow to speak.

If you aren't listening with an open mind and an open heart, you aren't really listening at all.

I don't think that having a conversation with others should always be about getting your own point across and being "right." By listening to others respectfully, and with an open mind, you may learn something, understand another side or perspective better, and if you are proven wrong, perhaps you could even *change your mind.*

Changing your mind takes grace and humility. But the reality is we are all wrong sometimes. We all have the wrong information sometimes that we're basing our opinions on. And none of us know everything about anything. We are all ignorant on something. Even experts in a certain field don't know everything there is to know about that topic.

So instead of being offended when someone has more knowledge about something than we do, what about getting excited to learn about it? What about graciously thanking them for teaching us something that changes our opinion on something?

It's okay to be wrong. It's okay to make mistakes. It's okay to fail. It's okay to admit you didn't know something. And it's okay to change your mind. It's all a part of the learning process.

It's okay not to change our opinions and values too, but it is very critical to the health of society that we find a way to listen, speak, and engage with others in a respectful and open manner. This takes maturity. It is also very positive.

It's perfectly okay to agree to disagree. However, it is not mature, positive, or healthy to cut people off who don't agree with you, and/or to engage in a verbal or physical argument over it.

Everyone has free will. Everyone can choose for themselves what they believe, value, and how they conduct their lives. Everyone gets to choose for themselves.

And if you think about it, this is part of what makes America great. Free speech. Free thinkers. Freedom. Liberty. The right to believe and practice what you believe in, in whatever way you so choose—so long as it does not break any laws or infringe on anyone else's rights.

But somewhere along the lines, many of us began to believe that everyone should think the way we do. That's not freedom. That's not respectful towards your fellow man. And that's not love.

God is love. And God shows us that a part of love is letting every person choose for themselves. He is not controlling or manipulative of anyone. Those qualities are not from God. They aren't a part of love.

Another aspect of being open, is not being so absolute and black and white about life. I know I have been very guilty of this at different times in my own life. What do I mean by this?

It is fanatical to say something has to be a certain way in order for us to be okay. After every break-up in my life, I told myself and others that I would never have love in my life again. That's fanatical, absolute, and not true.

We need to challenge our own belief systems that may be wrong. Many of are raised to believe lies. Even if our families didn't teach us lies, society as a whole, projects a lot of negative and mixed messages.

But we don't have to believe them. We can choose to believe something better, something more positive.

Some research shows that men prefer blondes, other research shows that men prefer brunettes. I've known men who prefer red heads. In reality, all women, and hair colors, and races, are beautiful in their own ways.

Everyone has their own preferences, and that's okay too, but what really matters is what's on the inside. Beauty defies age and hair color. Women and men of all hair colors find love. Nowadays, grey, silver, white, pink, blue, green, purple, and all shades therein are hair colors too. And they can all be absolutely beautiful.

Women and men of all shapes and sizes can be beautiful or handsome, and can be loved. Love is not about anything external—but the meeting of two souls who recognize in one another a perfect fit. Not that they, or any one of us perfect, but that they are perfect for each other.

We don't need a love relationship to complete us, but it is a beautiful gift in life to share love. Love, of course, can take many forms.

We can enjoy the love from our families, friends, our community, and even kindness or simple politeness from strangers. Even if we have no one close to us at the moment, we can have so much love in our hearts that our love is overflowing for others. We can always enjoy the love of a God who lives in us.

I have love and put love into every book I write. I put love into my service working feeding and clothing the homeless and families in need. I love everyone I meet. I am a people person! It is so positive to see the beauty, goodness, and special gifts in everyone we encounter.

I have found love so many times, but by thinking that my last love is my last love for life, is just wrong. The truth is, people find love all over the world in every way imaginable at any time in their life.

It's not about where you go, it's about becoming the best version of yourself in order to attract the people and things you really want.

It's about learning to truly love and appreciate yourself before finding your true love that will appreciate all you have to offer. It's about accepting that everyone is on their own journey with their own free will to make positive or negative choices for themselves. That is their right.

Their choices do affect you and others in their lives. So, we need to make our choices based on theirs. You could meet someone who you believe to be the love of your life. Then they could get into drugs, start stealing from you, lying to you, and mistreating you.

You remember how great it was in the beginning. You truly love them. But based on their choices, you can remove them from your life because their toxic behavior is hurting you.

It won't be easy, and in fact, it's heartbreaking. But if you want to live your best, most positive life, you will have to let some relationships go along the way.

Bestselling author and preacher Joyce Meyers says, (and this is paraphrased), "On the train of life, at every stop someone is going to have to get off!"

Not everyone we meet will stay with us throughout our whole lives. If nothing else, death will take them away. Death is a part of life. And it will come for all of us.

We have just one life to life, and it is our choice what we do with it.

It's always hard to lose anyone in our lives we have truly loved. To take a positive stanch, we can always be grateful for the time we shared, trusting that we will encounter new people in life who are more aligned to the person we are today.

It is not easy to stay positive. It is not easy to live your best life. But it is absolutely worth it.

If you *allow* people into your life who belittle you, abuse you, and mistreat you, it will affect you in negative ways. You can't be your best self if someone is telling you that you are worthless and ugly on a daily basis. Dr. Henry Cloud said, "You'll have what you tolerate."

I love to give this example of a science experiment that was done in the early 2000s. There were two plants in this study.

Both plants got the same amount of water and tending. But one plant was told every day how wonderful, beautiful, smart, good, and amazing they were. It flourished.

The second plant was told every day that they were horrible, ugly, stupid, bad, and just plain worthless. It wilted and died.

This proves the power of our words, even in nature, on two little plants. Can we even comprehend the power of our own words and the affect that it has on us and on others?

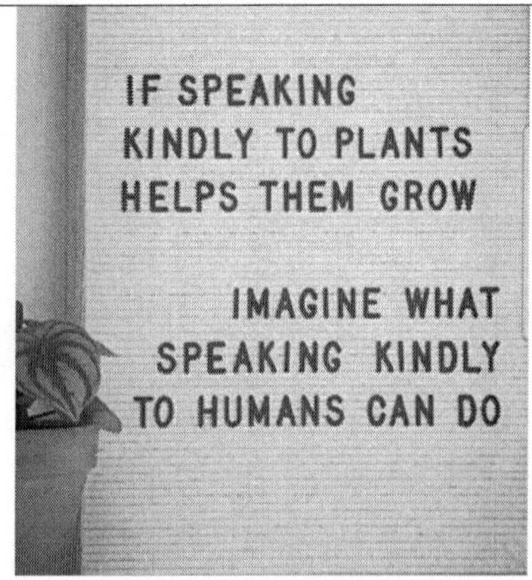

Use your words wisely. Words have the power of life and death. Words created life. And words can also destroy lives. Remember that when you speak to others, and also remember that in how you speak to yourself.

We can be our own worst enemies. Beating yourself up verbally doesn't help you or anyone else.

If you want to live your dreams and accomplish your goals, you've got to first believe in them, then claim it with your words, *as if you already have them.* Yes, words have power. So, let's use our words mindfully and wisely.

We can choose be open to the limitless possibilities of the universe. We can open ourselves to new ways of thinking, of living, of being. As we open ourselves up, we bloom like the lovely flowers of the spring.

Being open is very important to being positive. We don't need to know *how* something will occur. We just have to believe and have faith that it will. We have to be open to our dreams coming true in unexpected ways.

Instead of focusing on *how* you will achieve your goals, focus on preparing yourself so that you will be ready when the opportunities come. Focus on being in a state of grace in order to receive the blessings with open hands, and an open heart and mind.

Many things block our blessings from coming. One common thing that blocks our blessings is unforgiveness. If you are harboring hatred, resentment, and bitterness in your heart against someone that's like drinking poison every day and expecting to be healthy and blessed. That's like pouring gasoline over your garden and expecting your flowers to grow.

Being offended by others is actually a harm to yourself spiritually. If someone cuts you off in traffic, does it hurt them if you get angry? Do they hear you when you curse and scream and carry on? Would you really *want* them to hear you and be negatively affected by you?

What does it do to *you* when you get like that? Does your stomach hurt? Does your throat tighten? Do you feel nauseated or lightheaded? Does your heart quicken? Does your blood pressure rise?

Getting so angry over something so small is not healthy for anyone. *You* will feel the effects, not them.

Can you imagine that maybe they didn't mean to cut you off? Can you give them the benefit of the doubt?

Perhaps they don't know the area. Perhaps they are in an emergency, and were distracted. Should anyone be distracted when they drive?

No, but I would wager when you get the news that someone you love just died, or you just got fired, or something like that, you may be a bit off your game as you're driving home.

Doesn't it *feel* better to say. "Oh well, I'm sure they didn't mean to do that." And just get on with your day? Or not even give any attention to it at all?

Here's another aspect of being open. It's good to be open to the possibilities. But whatever opportunity you take, will close the door on another opportunity. You will never be able to go back, and take a different path. You can only do your best with the knowledge you have, and hope that the roads you take eventually get you to where you want to be.

I can give you an example from my own life. I had two possibilities of what to do one night in NYC. One was to go to a red-carpet event. I had wanted to do that all my life. The person going with me said there would be other opportunities to do that. There's wasn't. (Although life isn't over yet and I'm still hoping for the opportunity to attend many red-carpet events)!

The other option was the one I chose. It was a choice of sacrifice—to fight for those who had lost their voice. It was a public meeting for a homeless shelter coming into a community in Queens, set by the Department of Homeless Services. I went to the event to defend the homeless and represent my organization that was working to help them.

So, per usual, the meeting was bedlam. There were thousands of people screaming horrible things and acting more mentally ill than the homeless they claimed were crazy and mentally ill.

You had to sign up to speak for a minute and a half. Of course, everyone wanted to speak so there was supposed to be a limited time to speak, to try to give more people the opportunity to talk.

I did get to speak, but the brief time allotted me was cut off by the screaming I received as someone who was defending the homeless. I was one of only two speakers in defense of the homeless and helping them at that event. Everyone else was against them. They spoke for 5-15 minutes at a time, and because of their enraged behavior, they infringed on my time to speak.

Now was that fair? Not at all. So, I was told by the host, who was a very nice lady I knew from the Community Board 2, that I would be able to speak later on that night, but I wasn't able to because too many people wanted to speak.

Now, I have many dreams. One of them was to write for the New York Times, and of course, it would be wonderful to also be written about in it.

The room that night was full of reporters. One of them was from the New York Times. He asked me for a quote. But I was so upset about not getting to speak that I asked if I could email him a quote.

He gave his email, and I did email him a quote, but he never spoke to me again. Maybe I missed that brief opportunity. Maybe he could see how upset I was and it turned him off and he didn't want to deal with it—me.

So, I missed out on two important opportunities that night, a red-carpet event that would have made *me* immensely happy to attend, and may have led to acting opportunities, or at least auditions, and being quoted in the New York Times, which would no doubt have elevated my work with the homeless in some way.

I will never know what could have happened that night if I had put a smile on my face, shook my head at the chaos, and taken the opportunity to use my voice to be quoted in the New York Times—for the sake of the homeless and hungry.

But instead of dwelling in the past, being full of regret and despair, I choose to believe and be open to the fact that more opportunities *will* come. And next time, I'll do my best to be ready for them.

I can still go to auditions. I can still (and have) been quoted in almost a hundred newspapers, magazines, podcasts, radio, and TV Shows—so far. Not the New York Times—yet. I have certainly missed out on some opportunities, and I am learning from those mistakes.

Boy, am I grateful for everything that has worked out too. All the millions of people I have helped through my nonprofit. I hope to help so many more.

I am learning to not get caught up in the drama. Sometimes I still do, but not as much. I'm making progress. That's the best we all can do. Make progress.

To live your best life, it is best to remove yourself from the chaos. I have not achieved all of my dreams, but I am infinitely grateful for the dreams that have come true.

I am infinitely grateful for how far I have come. I believe that the best of life is still ahead of me. I hope that's true for everyone reading this.

They say the only reason to look down on someone is to help them up. The same can be said for your own life. We've all made mistakes. We all missed out on opportunities because we didn't recognize them in the moment or we allowed ourselves to be in a negative state of mind so that we were unable to receive the blessings intended for us.

But here's the silver lining: more opportunities will come. They will keep coming. There is still time to get things right.

If you have a destiny, the universe will give you chance after chance to achieve it. It is never too late. It can still happen. *Always.*

Ways to Become More Open

- Work on your self-confidence. Ways to do so: self-care, wear a nice outfit, make a doctor's appointment to alleviate a health problem, buy yourself a nice meal, take a hot bubble bath, pamper yourself sometimes!
- Opening up is all about being comfortable in your own skin. Believe in yourself and others will too.
- Practice being vulnerable and opening up more in relationships and on social media when safe and if you feel led to do so.
- Find common ground and shared interests with people you meet.
- Adopt an attitude of curiosity when you meet people who are different from you in some way. Ask them questions with the intention to get to know them and understand them better.
- Get out of your comfort zone. Go to new places and try new things.
- Say what's truly on your mind and heart. Be honest and sincere in your dealings.
- Use "I" statements. Example: "I really enjoy hanging out with you." "I'm so glad we decided to try this new restaurant out!" Instead of, "Are you happy to be here?" and "Do you enjoy hanging out with me?"
- Process and work through any problems in your past that may be affecting your ability to be open to life today. For instance, if a friend betrayed you, you may have developed trust issues. It is very important to work through those issues so

that it doesn't block you from having healthier, more positive relationships now and in the future. If you need help to process your emotions, seek a counselor or trusted advisor who can help guide you through it in a healthy way.

Being open can be trying new foods that titillate the taste buds. You can feast on new concepts that excite you and expand your mind. You can be open to new cultures that teach you new concepts that make you a more well-rounded person.

You can find new friends, and learn from and appreciate their differences. You can meet new people. You can go new places. You can explore new lands that capture your imagination with their beauty.

You can try to do new things, and some of them you may even find that you love, and brings you so much joy—that you never would have experienced, if you hadn't been open to it. You can expand your horizons in any number of ways, simply by being open to them.

PRACTICAL APPLICATION
For Positive Openness

Prayer

Please help me Lord, to see others through your eyes. Help to recognize that you created them and you love them as much you love me. Help me to be open to what they have to teach me. Help me to be open to helping them however I can. Help me to be willing to be a miracle for them, just as I want and need miracles in my life as well.

Meditation: Meditate 10 minutes today on how you on can radically accept where you're at in life. Start with 10 deep breaths. Feel your body relax. Then imagine your mind as a window or door, with light flooding from it, and through it.

Picture people coming together of all looks and cultures, sitting together and discussing ideas, without judgment, blame, interruptions, or disrespect. Imagine them all sharing their own unique and exotic foods, how exciting it can be to try new things. Imagine you find a food you like, and feel your heart and mind expand to realize if you weren't open to these people, you never would have discovered this delicious new cuisine!

Imagine learning something new by exchanging ideas, and teaching someone else there something new. Hold on to the feeling of excitement, joy, pleasure or whatever other emotions come up at the positive experience that being open to other people and things created in your life. Visualize your world expanding, as you evolve by being open.

Affirmations

I am open to possibilities.

I am unlimited.

I choose to live my life unoffended.

I choose to be open to other people's thoughts and ideas without being threatened or afraid of them.

I am open to my problems being solved without me trying to control the situation.

I am open to life.

I am open to others.

I respect the opinions of others.

I am open to being wrong and making mistakes in order to learn from them.

Declarations

I know that the Lord has plans for me, plans for my good, to give me hope and a future. (Adapted from Jeremiah 29:11, ESV)

I was called to freedom. I will use my freedom to serve others through love. (Adapted from Galatians 5:13)

I am a prisoner of hope. God will restore me double for what I have lost. (Adapted from Zechariah 9:12)

Song

"Live Like You Were Dying"
By Tim Nichols and Craig Wiseman

Said I was in my early 40's
With a lot of life before me
When a moment came that stopped me on a dime
I spent most of the next days, lookin' at the x-rays
Talkin' 'bout the options and talkin' 'bout sweet time
Asked when it sank in
That this might really be the real end
How's it hit ya, when you get that kind of news
Man what ya do
And he says

I went sky divin'
I went Rocky Mountain climbin'
I went 2.7 seconds on a bull name Fu Manchu
And I loved deeper
And I spoke sweeter
And I gave forgiveness I'd been denying
And he said someday I hope you get the chance
To live like you were dyin'

She said I was finally the husband
That most the time I wasn't
And I became a friend a friend would like to have
And all a sudden goin' fishing
Wasn't such an imposition
And I went three times that year I lost my dad
Well, I finally read the good book
And I took a good long hard look at what I'd do
If I could do it all again
And then

I went sky divin'
I went Rocky Mountain climbin'

I went 2.7 seconds on a bull name Fu Manchu
And I loved deeper
And I spoke sweeter
And I gave forgiveness I'd been denying
And he said someday I hope you get the chance
To live like you were dyin'

Like tomorrow was gift and you've got eternity
To think about what to do with it
What could you do with it, what can
I do with it, what would I do with it

Sky divin'
I went Rocky Mountain climbin'
I went 2.7 seconds on a bull name Fu Manchu
And I loved deeper
And I spoke sweeter
And I watched an eagle as it was flying
And he said someday I hope you get the chance
To live like you were dyin'

CHAPTER SIX
Positivity is About Focus

Think about positivity like a muscle. What you use will grow. If you consciously think of ways to see things in life as positive, you will start to find the positive in every situation. It will become a habit.

What you focus on you will find.

It's the same with exercise. If you don't get out there and move your muscles they will atrophy, becoming weak and flabby. As they say, "Use it or lose!"

Positivity is about finding and focusing on the good in everything and everyone. This includes yourself. If you know who you are, and you have nothing to prove to yourself or anyone else, that's living your best life.

Positivity is not about ignoring problems. It's about FACING THEM. But you don't have to focus on your problems so much that you stop enjoying your life.

In relationships and for self-improvement, it's good to focus on the positive, while working to improve the negative. People need encouragement in order to change. But this book is not about changing other people—it's about changing and bettering ourselves.

We can't change or control anybody else. Nor should we. You can't help someone who isn't willing to help themselves. And you can't want a better life for someone else, more than they want it for themselves.

I've had to learn that the hard way. Many times, over and over. Often well-meaning people become enablers for other people's bad habits and choices.

It doesn't work.

When I finally accepted that I can't save anyone else from themselves, I began to heal myself from this toxic pattern. I stopped trying to change them, and focused on changing myself. When I cut those people from my life, I saw tremendous growth in every area of my life.

I was happier than I'd ever been. And that's when the healing could really begin in.

You can't heal yourself of negative patterns, while you're in a toxic relationship. You need to first remove the cancer from your body, before your scars from that wound can begin to heal.

What you focus on grows. What you think about, you will often attract. We can focus on what we have, or what we don't have. We will be happy, healthier people if we focus on what we do have. This is our choice to make. Every day of our lives. Every moment.

If we focus on all the negative aspects of our past relationships, unfortunately, that makes us more likely to attract more of the same. If you're in a relationship and you're constantly telling the other person what you don't like about them, that doesn't motivate them to improve. If you tell yourself how horrible you are for your own bad habits, that negative focus will probably not lead to a positive result.

When we try to control others, and the situation we're in, that never really works. The only thing we truly have control over is ourselves—and we're hard enough to control!

Focusing on other people's problems is a savvy way to avoid our own. But it's a lot healthier to focus on self-improvement then on fixing the problems of those around us. Ultimately, we show others love, respect, and grace by allowing them to make their own mistakes, and either learn from them or deteriorate or waste their lives.

That is their choice to make. Love it not about control. If they want to waste their life, and make bad decision after bad decision, that it is their choice to make and their life to waste.

However, we get to decide who we let into our lives, and who we allow to be close to us. If someone you love is making bad choices, that will negatively affect you in some way. You are well within your rights to tell that person goodbye. Because unfortunately, on some level we do become like the company we keep. Or at the very least, even if they don't corrupt us, they will destroy us, and our lives.

I'm sorry to tell you, but you are not going to go where you want to go, and become your best self with toxic people in your life. If you want to have your best life, letting people go is usually a necessary sacrifice.

Of course, not everyone has toxic people in their lives. Every one and every case is different. I can just tell you, go with your gut. It's almost always right, and it's better to be safe than sorry.

People are bound to say and do things that hurt us. Sometimes we hurt others too, whether we mean to or not.

When we make a mistake, we will have to reap the consequences of it. When we choose to learn from our mistakes, then we are focusing on the positive, and something positive results from something bad.

Instead of focusing on failures and mistakes, and beating ourselves up over them, why don't we see those things as a good thing, as learning experiences? There's going to be a next time. There's going to be more chances to get things right. When you know better, you do better. So, in that sense, making mistakes is a good thing, and it is a necessary part of the path that leads to success.

Our next blessing comes after the last storm, test, trial, or sacrifice.

We need to find a way to enjoy ourselves in the "mean" time. We shouldn't ignore our problems, but we also shouldn't let them become the main focus of our lives.

Instead of focusing on the problem, we need to remind ourselves that God is bigger than our problems. We need to remember that God is in control.

We need to remember all the storms that God has brought us through. He is our rock in whatever storm we face, as in the next illustration.

The storms will pass. The seasons will come and go. As will many people in our lives. What remains, is what we've learned, and what we've endured that built us into the powerhouse we become. What remains, are our values, our beliefs, and those things we find worth fighting for: a cause, a dream, a love that stands the test of time, and all the tests along the way.

We can let the pain break us. Or can choose to do the hard work required to repair ourselves, and put all those broken pieces back together again.

There are things that remain true forever. There are things that can never be broken or destroyed. Like faith, hope, and love. They are eternal. As are our souls.

We all have positive things to focus on. So, keep your eyes on the prize, while working to hit smaller goals along the way.

I'm not advocating avoiding your problems. I'm advocating a balance between focusing on your problems—and driving yourself (and those around you) crazy trying to solve them. Been there, done that. It doesn't help. I'm focusing on finding a way to celebrate my life even in the midst of the storms and problems.

Believe me, I understand how hard it can be to strike this balance. I've often been on either side of the pendulum. I'm still working towards a balance. But I'm learning that rest after hard work, often fosters *more* creativity and productivity then if you just keep forcing yourself to plow ahead like a work horse.

Resting and taking breaks is imperative to having positive results. It can actually help your mind come up with brilliant and innovative solutions, by resting your brain. Trust the process. *Enjoy* the process.

The mind is not meant to go 50 miles an hour, 24 hours a day, 7 days a week. That will make anyone goofy.

Taking breaks, taking time off, taking a nap, relaxing, taking a vacation, getting your mind off your problems—are all ways to help renew your mind, so that you can come back to your problems, and tackle them with a fresh new perspective. Often out-of-the-blue, while you're focusing your mind on something you enjoy, the answers you've been searching for will pop into your mind, seemingly effortlessly.

Or, your problem will come to resolution without you. That's when you know it's from God, and that He answered your prayers. More than likely any solution from God will be much better than anything we could have come up with ourselves.

Let's talk about some health benefits of positivity. A recent study published in the American Journal of Epidemiology in 2017, followed 70,000 women from 2004 to 2012 and found that those who were optimistic had a significantly lower risk of dying from several major causes of death, including:

- Heart disease

- Stroke
- Infections
- Respiratory Diseases
- Cancer (including breast, ovarian, colorectal and lung cancers)

Other proven benefits of thinking positively include:

- better quality of life
- higher energy levels
- better psychological and physical health
- faster recovery from injury or illness
- fewer colds
- lower rates of depression
- better stress management and coping skills
- longer life span

Positive thinking isn't magic and it isn't a magical cure to make all of your problems go away. What it will do is make problems more manageable, and help you approach hardships in a more productive way.

When we've done all that we can do, it's important to cast your cares upon God, trusting that He will work everything out, often better than we ever could have imagined. You can find peace in knowing that you did your part.

Focus. Focus. Focus. Focus.

For those of us with a lot of energy, or for anyone really, focus is the key to productivity. If you have a dream, or purpose (and we all do, we just have to discover it), then the truth is, while there are those who manifest it all in an instant, most of us will need to take small, practical steps to get us where we want to go. Focus is critical in getting us there.

If you focus on when you *don't* want, unfortunately, whether you intend to our not, you will probably create more of it. Creating what you *do* want will require your focus.

Visualizing having what you want, praying about it, making a vision board, and meditating on it, are ways to help you manifest your dreams. Making a list of some practical steps towards your goals and then doing them, will help get you there sooner.

At the root of getting what we want is our emotions. Our feelings of deservability, and focusing on what we *have,* rather than what we *lack,* immediately, magically, creates more of what we *want.*

It's true. Positive thinking + positive emotions + positive actions = the manifestation of what we desire. By focusing on the positive it creates more positives in our lives.

Of course, nothing is ever quite so simple or cut and dry. Our lives are all different of course. We are individuals with life experiences personal to us. But in essence, this is the recipe for success.

When we focus on what we have, spiritually, the universe will give us more of it. When we focus on what we don't have, spiritually, we are more likely to lose more of what we have.

There are spiritual lessons in life. There is an evolution of the soul. As we learn these concepts and principles, as we live them out, we rise higher in the spiritual realm, and also in our success in life.

When our focus is on the positive, the negative won't have as much power over us. Our problems seem smaller when we contemplate the majesty of the rising and setting sun, the magnificence of the moon and stars, the miracle of every human being on earth, who was born for a special purpose.

You are a miracle. I am a miracle. Everyone who is ever born on this earth is a miracle. Life is a miracle. And life is a gift.

It doesn't always feel that way. Sometimes it feels like a burden. I validate that feeling. I have it sometimes too. Yet the more you create positive experiences for yourself, the more beautiful and positive life can become.

You have a purpose. Focus on that.

No matter what curve balls life throws your way, if you get up every morning and take steps towards achieving your goals, eventually you *will* achieve them. You will also have overcome a lot of tests and challenges along the way, through right focus.

Your positive focus will no doubt enrich the lives of everyone around you. You will win friends and popularity, and you'll be happy in your times of solitude and reflection too.

Focus on the positive, and watch as more positive things come your way. Focus on the negative, and soon you will be blinded by the darkness of negativity and regret.

We all have a reason to be bitter and angry—but that's no reason to be bitter and angry. Allow yourself to feel that anger and bitterness, then find a healthy, and a meaningful way to you, to let it go.

If you focus on what brings you joy and happiness, and you let that joy and happiness in, you will become a truly positive person, who makes the world a better, brighter place, simply by being in it.

PRACTICAL APPLICATION
For Positive Focus

Prayer

Thank you, Lord, for all that you have given me. I do not deserve all the good you have given me, but I am very grateful for it. I have so many blessings. Help me to focus on my blessings and everything I have to be grateful for.

Help me to take my eyes off my problems and circumstances and fix them on you. Help me to seek you with all my heart, mind, body, soul, and spirit. Help me to remember in the midst of the storm, that you are good, that you care, and that this too shall pass.

No matter how difficult life can be, you love me, and I believe that you will turn things around. Not in my time, not in my way, but I believe that your way and your timing will be better than I ever could have imagined, or come up with myself.

I believe that good things are in store for me, and that the best is yet to come. Help me to focus on all the times you've come through for me, provided for me, and answered my prayers. Help me to remember and focus on those times, knowing that you hear my prayers, that you love me and that you care. Amen.

Meditation: Meditate 10 minutes today on at least one major things God has provided for you. Examples: your home, your food, any success or door that He has opened that you could not have opened on your own.

Affirmations

Today I am choosing to focus on what I have. I have so much to be thankful for.

I am focusing on all the good things I like about myself and others.

I choose to dwell on all my blessings.

I choose to remember all the times my prayers were answered.

I am encouraged when others share their testimonies about how you have blessed them in their lives. It reminds me that you have blessed me, and will bless me again.

I choose to focus on what I have control over.

I choose to focus on all the good things happening in life.

I am focused on the beauty of life.

Today, I am choosing to focus on the positive.

Declarations

I choose to think about what is true, what is honorable, what is just, what is noble, what is pure, what is lovely, what is commendable, what is excellent, and anything and everything that is worthy of praise. (Adapted from Philippians 4:8)

I delight myself in the Lord, and as I do, He gives me the desires of my heart. (Adapted from Psalm 37:4)

I seek first the Kingdom of God, and His righteousness. (Adapted from Matthew 6:33)

Song

"Count Your Blessings"
By Johnson Oatman Jr.

When upon life's billows you are tempest-tossed,
When you are discouraged, thinking all is lost,
Count your many blessings, name them one-by-one,
And it will surprise you what the Lord has done.

Count your blessings, name them one-by-one,
Count your blessings, see what God has done!
Count your blessings, name them one-by-one,
Count your many blessings, see what God has done.
And it will surprise you what the Lord has done.

Are you ever burdened with a load of care?
Does the cross seem heavy you are called to bear?
Count your many blessings, every doubt will fly,
And you will keep singing as the days go by.

When you look at others with their lands and gold,
Think that Christ has promised you His wealth untold;
Count your many blessings—money cannot buy—
wealth can never buy
Your reward in heaven, nor your home on high.

So, amid the conflict whether great or small,
Do not be discouraged, God is over all;
Count your many blessings, angels will attend,
Help and comfort give you to your journey's end.

CHAPTER SEVEN
Positivity is About Growth

What I'm about to say may sound trite. When you're in the thick of it, trying not to drown in the storms of life, it can even feel insensitive, but it really is true: there is a lesson in everything.

There is a positive way to look at the difficulties in your life. When you get to the point of asking yourself, "What can I learn from this situation?" Then you know you are ready to grow.

The truth is, once you learn your lesson, you can move on from it—to other, harder lessons! *Ha!*

The universe will probably give you more tests in the same category or type of scenario, to see if you have *really* learned your lesson or not. If you have, then there will be new, harder tests and trials. But you will have learned the positive way of handling it.

It is important to understand that these lessons are intended to help us to grow, to make us better people, and once we have passed them, we will graduate into living our best lives.

We have to endure the bitter to get to the sweet. Time heals all wounds. But only if we do the work necessary to learn our lessons. Only then can we truly move on from them.

Toxic people block our blessings and stunt our growth. It's like they're blocking out the sun, denying us nurturing water, and encouraging the weeds of our bad habits to take root. It's like they're a poison that is slowly killing us. Or ivy that is slowly choking us out.

If you're a toxic person yourself, you don't have to be. Bad habits can be broken. You can replace a bad habit with a good one in 30 days research shows. Instead of doing drugs, you can pray. You can exercise. You can trade in toxic behaviors and people in your life for positive ones.

In some way, we all have our own brand of negativity that stems from our pain and traumatic experiences. Not one of us is ever going to be 100% positive 100% of the time. That would be an unreasonable expectation.

But as you become a healthier person, and find the strength and resolve to cut away the toxic people and bad habits from your life, there will probably be a time of emptying out. This is also a test to see if you will go back to the negative out of loneliness or fear.

Fear that you will never have anything better. Fear that you will never have what you really want. That you *can't* have it.

As you begin a healthier routine, you may experience a void that sometimes makes you feel sad and alone. That's okay. Lean into it. This time on our own is necessary for our healing and our growth.

The universe doesn't allow voids for long. This is only a moment in time. Things are bound to change—you can either grow and become better, or you can go back to your old ways, and watch as your life gets worse all over again. Or you can stand still, stuck waiting, without the actions necessary to attain the positive growth and change you seek.

We all have moments of weakness. We have to learn to get through them, without trying to go back to the comfortable, the familiar, the not-the-best for us. We have to learn to say *no* to what we *don't* want in order to eventually attract what we *do* want.

There is a power in NO. And by saying NO, you are showing the universe that you will no longer settle for anything less than *everything.*

If you *do* go back to your old routines and your old ways, try not to be too hard on yourself. It is common to go back and forth in the process of change and growth. We've all been there. You're not alone in this. For most of us, it takes making some mistakes to grow. Most would say you are BOUND to fail at times in order to grow and attain success.

If you're able to quit a relationship or habit like smoking, cold turkey, more power to you. But most people will smoke a few more cigarettes several more times in the process of trying to quit.

That's okay. Please try to show compassion for yourself. What you're doing isn't easy. But if you keep pushing through, you'll be better for it.

Blame and judgement won't help yourself or anyone else. Positive self-talk will. Keep telling yourself that you can overcome this habit, and you *will* overcome it.

Because you CAN doing anything you set your mind to. *That's the truth!*

What's important when you fall down (because we all fall down) is that you get back on the horse, and you try again. Eventually, you will overcome anything—as long as *you never give up!*

Think about how you would talk to a beloved child or a best friend. Then speak to yourself with the same degree of caring, gentleness, and respect.

Would you tell a child they aren't good enough? Would you tell them that they aren't pretty or handsome enough? Would you call people you love fat, worthless, stupid and however else you put down yourself?

Of course, narcissists think very highly of themselves, and actually, their growth is more about becoming humbler.

But for the good people out there who are their own worst enemy, if you want your life to get better, you need to *feel* better, and *think* better, and *talk* to yourself better.

Just as, if you're trying to get healthier, you eat more fruits and vegetables—if you want to become more healthy, positive, and successful, you're going to need to build yourself up, from the inside.

Once we understand and identify which distortions show up in our thinking, we can counter them with more positive thoughts. Below is a list of 10 common cognitive distortions.

Always Being Right: Similar to how it sounds, when we engage in this distortion, we believe we're always right and will argue with people who think otherwise. Example: *I'm going to win this argument because I'm always right.*

Blaming: Blaming is when we either blame others for our emotional pain or blame ourselves. Example: *You're the reason I had a bad day! It's* ***your*** *fault!*

Catastrophizing: Also known as "magnifying," catastrophizing is when we exaggerate the negative details of an event, making them a much bigger deal than they are. Example: *I failed that test—what if I flunk out of school?*

Control Fallacies: There are two types of control fallacies. If we believe we are externally controlled, we perpetually see ourselves as the victim of external forces. If we believe we have internal control, we imagine that other people feel a certain way (pain, happiness, sadness, etc.) because of something we did. Example: *Are you mad because of something I said?*

Emotional Reasoning: Emotional reasoning is when we believe that everything we feel must be true. Example: *I feel guilty, therefore I must be a bad person.*

Filtering: Mental filtering is when we filter out the positives of a situation and only focus on the negative. Example: *That student left during my presentation, therefore my presentation was bad.*

Jumping to Conclusions (Making Assumptions): We jump to conclusions when we make a hasty judgment or believe something to be true without bothering to consider all the facts. Example: *She gave me a funny look. I think she hates me.*

Overgeneralization: Overgeneralization is when we conclude that because of one bad experience, all experiences related to that will be bad. Example: *I failed that test. This is going to be a horrible term.*

Personalization: This is a cognitive distortion where we take everything personally and compare ourselves to others. Example: *He made that comment in class just to get at me.*

Polarized Thinking: Also known as "black-and-white" thinking, polarized thinking is when we believe there is no middle ground—either something is perfect or a failure. Example: *I missed that one question, so I did badly on the test.*

We can train ourselves to be more positive and have positive thinking. It's all about our focus. Below are some steps on how to retrain your negative thinking.

8 Steps to Retrain Your Brain to Curb Negative Thoughts

1. Develop a Morning Routine.
2. Switch Up Your Environment.
3. Practice Daily Gratitude.
4. Be More Aware of Your Thoughts.
5. Create a Personal Mantra.
6. Understand What Triggers You.
7. Turn Negatives into Positives.
8. Pay It Back. Pay it Forward.

We're all going to change. We need to accept that. But the positive thing is that we get to decide if that change is going to be good or bad. We get decide if we will grow, get stuck, or get worse.

There are those who say, "Accept me as I am, I'm never going to change." But nature shows us that every day change is inevitable, both outside of us and within us.

Some people grow up, some people grow out, and some people get worse. But one way or another, we are all going to change.

Growth is one step (or one giant leap of faith) outside of your comfort zone, as in the illustration below.

Outside of us, we cannot control our circumstances or what the people in our lives choose to do. We do not control the weather, and the devastation of natural disasters.

We may experience problems and even devastation in our own lives that we didn't cause, and that may not be fair, but we still have to deal with it *if* we want to keep moving forward in a positive way.

There are spiritual lessons to be gleaned even in the most terrible of circumstances. The following are some examples of some valuable lessons I've learned so far in life. These are lessons I learned that caused me a lot of pain, but that ultimately helped me to grow.

- Death can teach us to appreciate our lives more, appreciate others more, and to live our lives to the fullest.
- Loss can teach us to appreciate what we have, and not take it for granted.
- Taking responsibility for our lives and our problems, empowers us, and takes back our control. Whereas, blaming someone else gives them the power, and makes you a victim all over again.
- Devastation shows us that we are strong enough to start again, start over, build something valuable from the ground up, over and over again, for as many times as it takes to build something really special that will last the test of time.
- Learning to praise God in the hard times unlocks miracles and blessings.
- Praying for those who have hurt you, used you, lied about you, abused you, and hurt you in some way can be healing for them and for you. It can turn them into a friend, and at the very least, unlocks your own blessings. If you curse others, you are really cursing yourself.
- Forgiving others sets you free.
- Seeing the best in others brings out their best.
- Treat *yourself* how you want to be treated.

There are many things we do not have control over in life. Most things. We can work to control ourselves, and use our circumstances, both good and bad, to foster our personal growth.

Why not embrace the change? Why not become resilient to learn new skill sets and concepts in a constantly changing world? Why not evolve? Why not improve with age, inside and out?

Why can't we become more fit at 60 than we were at 20? We can! Why not stay fit our whole lives? *We can!* Anything is possible, if we believe, and are committed to our growth.

We can study all our lives, any science under the sun. We can learn something new every day. We can learn *ten* new things every day! Our minds can become sharper as we age. *If we use them.*

We *can* grow our muscles by using them. We can improve our IQ and our knowledge through study and accessing different parts of our brain to keep it strong, like regularly doing puzzles, reading, or Sudoku.

We can evolve our souls through spiritual practices such as prayer, reading the Bible, service and volunteer work, and most importantly, by trying to live out the beautiful, holy principles therein.

We can evolve our hearts through the power of forgiveness and radical acceptance of the things in our life we cannot change. When we release our anger, bitterness, and resentment, and exchange it for compassion, mercy, and forgiveness, we are exercising our heart muscle and we grow and evolve in our emotions. That affects our bodies too.

Our bodies and minds are not independent of each other. It is imperative to take a holistic approach to our healing. It is important to understand that physical components affect the emotional, the mental, and the spiritual. Everything is connected.

Something as simple as getting enough sleep, and keeping a balanced, healthy diet, can affect your mood. Every single type of food is composed of properties that either add to your life, or take away from it.

You are what you eat.

By the same token, if you think more positively, that will positively affect your emotions and your health. It all goes hand-in-hand.

We can exercise our muscles in order to become more fit and healthy. We can exchange negative coping mechanisms for healthy ones. Focus is certainly an important part of practicing mindfulness. Then the inevitable changes that life brings are more likely to be positive.

Steps Towards Positive Growth

1.) Take an online or college class, or any type of class which helps you to learn a new skill.
2.) Read more books.
3.) Watch educational television.
4.) Study, learn, and practice a new language.
5.) Go someplace you've never been on your own.
6.) Cultivate a talent.
7.) Learn a musical instrument. Join a band!
8.) Start your own business or nonprofit.
9.) Champion and advocate for a person, organization, or a cause you believe in.
10.) Engage in service works that feeds your soul and helps others or your community.
11.) Commit to an exercise routine.
12.) Start and/or end the day with gratitude.
13.) Eat healthier.

14.) Cook more. If you don't know how to cook, take a cooking class, or buy some cookbooks! It's usually healthier to prepare your meals at home.

15.) Watch positive videos on YouTube, podcasts, etc.

16.) Learn to rest and take breaks.

17.) Learn to meditate and make that a daily ritual.

18.) Go to the doctor when needed.

19.) Improve sleep.

20.) Reduce stress and anxiety.

21.) Lengthen your attention span.

22.) Enhance self-awareness.

23.) Trade bad habits for good ones.

24.) Work on memory tools to improve your mind and keep it strong and sharp.

25.) Use skills, and if necessary, medication, to regulate your emotions. Be aware of and work on your mental health. Positive thinking is a great way to start!

Growth is all about change, self-improvement, and transforming and becoming a better version of yourself. Just as a caterpillar completely changes form to become the butterfly, so can we, spiritually.

The caterpillar must go through a period of great struggle to break through its cocoon. This gives him the strength to beat his new wings and learn to fly.

As humans, it is usually a *break down* that proceeds a *breakthrough.* We have to go through hardships in order to handle our greatest hopes and desires and dreams.

Lean into what you are going through. Whatever you resist, persists. Instead, learn how to go *through* it.

Believe you are strong enough to handle whatever you face. Because you ARE. The universe would not have given you this challenge if you weren't.

We are never given more than we can handle. It sure feels that way sometimes, though, doesn't it?

But by going *through* things, we grow in ways we couldn't have imagined. And the fact is, we wouldn't grow without the pain.

They call it "growing pains" for a reason.

The same is true of our dreams. The universe would not give you a dream, if it wasn't meant to come true.

The key is to understand that great things often take work and time. You will probably have to sacrifice a lot, and learn and grow a lot, in order to live that dream.

But just as a caterpillar, crawling on its belly on the ground, like a slimy slug, or a slithering snake, can struggle through its cocoon in its metamorphous and transform into the colorful butterfly that grows wings to fly, so can we metamorphous and grow, into absolutely anything we want to be.

If you dream it, you CAN achieve it. You'll just have to grow into it.

PRACTICAL APPLICATION
For Positive Growth

Prayer

Dear Lord, I trust you to help me to change in the areas of my life that I need to. I recognize that we all have room for improvement and growth. Help me to grow into the person you want me to be.

Please give me to have discernment in how I may become the person you have created me to be. Help me to blossom and flourish in the fruits of the spirit, so that my life can be a wellspring of blessings for myself and for those who cross my path. Amen.

Meditation: Meditate 10 minutes today on one bad habit you once had that you were able to overcome.

Affirmations

I am ready to learn.

I am prepared to grow.

I am excited to change.

I am thrilled to expand.

I choose to improve myself.

I am constantly evolving.

I am able.

I am capable.

I am ready to accept all the good that the universe has in store for me.

Declarations

I am a new creation in Christ. The old has passed away; the new has come. (Adapted from 2 Corinthians 5:17)

LORD, you are my Father. I am the clay, and you are my potter. I am the work of your hands. (Adapted from Isaiah 64:8)

I have sinned and fallen short of the glory of God. We all have sinned and fallen short of His glory. But we are justified by his gift of grace, through the redemption of Jesus Christ and the blood He shed on the cross, which I receive by faith. (Adapted from Romans 3:23-24)

Song

"For Good"
From Wicked

I've heard it said,
That people come into our lives,
For a reason.
Bringing something we must learn.
And we are led to those
Who help us most to grow—if we let them,
And we help them in return.

Well, I don't know if I believe that's true.
But I know I'm who I am today,
Because I knew you.

Like a comet pulled from orbit,
As it passes a sun.

Like a stream that meets a boulder,
Halfway through the wood.
Who can say if I've been changed for the better,
But because I knew you,
I have been changed for good.

It well may be,
That we will never meet again,
In this lifetime.
So let me say before we part,
So much of me,
Is made of what I learned from you.
You'll be with me,
Like a hand print on my heart.
And now whatever way our stories end,
I know you have rewritten mine,
By being my friend.
Like a ship blown from its mooring,
By a wind off the sea.
Like a sea dropped by a sky bird,
In a distant wood.
Who can say if I've been changed for the better,
But because I knew you

Because I knew you
I have been changed for good.

And just to clear the air,
I ask forgiveness,
For the things I've done,
You blamed me for.

But then,
I guess,

We know there's blame to share.
And none of it seems to matter,
Anymore.

Like a comet pulled from orbit
(Like a ship blown from its mooring,)
As it passes a sun.
(By a wind off the sea.)
Like a stream that meets a boulder,
(Like a sea dropped by sky bird,)
Halfway through the wood.
(In the wood.)
Who can say if I've been changed for the better.
I do believe I have been changed for the better.

And because I knew you
Because I knew you,
Because I knew you,
I have been changed
For good.

CHAPTER EIGHT
Positivity is About Action

Action Steps Towards a More Positive Life

1.) Get out of your comfort zone.
2.) Compliment and encourage yourself and others.
3.) Stop slouching. Sit, and stand up, straight and tall. Hold your head up high. Shoulders back. This makes you appear confident.
4.) Ask for and accept help when you need it.
5.) Help others when you can.
6.) Accept and love others for who they are and where they're at.
7.) Accept and love yourself for who you are.
8.) Write down your goals and make action steps towards achieving them every day.
9.) Celebrate the victories—great and small.
10.) Get an accountability partner who challenges you to be and do your best.
11.) Never quit, give in, or give up!

This is the point when we take the first 7 principles of positivity we have learned and apply them into positive action. Now we work towards our goals.

People can support you. But no one can rescue or save you. Only God saves. We can learn how to rescue ourselves.

Nothing is every 100% someone else's fault, OR our fault. By figuring out how we can do better in any given situation, we empower ourselves to do better next time.

Every step we take can be a step forward, and a step in the right direction. Every day we can work towards living a more positive, happier life.

I once had a talented friend named Jerry Drake, who told me that the best time to start or do anything is right **now**, as in the illustration below.

I think it's apropos that the man who shared this valuable piece of wisdom with me, has since passed away.

We only have this moment. And what we do with it will affect our future—tomorrow, and years to come.

It will also affect the legacy we leave behind, after we are gone.

Many of us start off in life with a bad childhood. Many of us make mistakes in our lives, throughout our adulthood. Many of us choose the wrong jobs, the wrong people to surround ourselves with, and make poor decisions.

That's great! Why? Because you can learn from those things, and take what you've learned to help others. You can take all those mistakes and turn them into positive action.

You may have to do the right thing for a long time before you see positive results, but do not give up! At the right time you will reap the rewards—in God's time.

But only if you persist when the chips are down and the times are tough. Only if you continue to think positive and speak positive things into existence. If you go back to your old, negative ways, patterns, and habits, you can expect the same results.

You can expect not to grow. You can expect to get stuck, like a pig in the mud. You will not forward.

But guess what? Negative patterns can be changed into healthy patterns. Bad habits can be turned into healthy habits. By our actions!

Instead of staying in the habit of smoking with your cofree in the morning, you can set your intention for a great day with positive affirmations, morning meditation, prayer, and/or a daily devotional, and just see how much better your day goes!

Even when you start your day "right," things outside of your control can still go wrong. These positive actions will, at the very least, enable you to cope with them better. So, either way, doing these positive things will help you to deal with your problems better, and eventually, to overcome them.

It's always so much fun to start something isn't it? It's so fun to start a new project. But it's how we finish that really matters.

Seeing your dreams come true takes action, hard work, discipline and the perseverant stick-to-itiveness that is necessary for any accomplishment. It takes a lot of testing to develop the qualities needed for success.

Anyone can develop these qualities at any time in their lives. When is the best time to start again? As Jerry Drake would say—right NOW!

Your history does not have to be your future. Your past does not have to control your future. By letting go of the past, and what you cannot control, you move forward.

You can still have a fantastic finish in life, no matter how you began.

Right actions take courage. Being brave means doing it afraid. We cannot do anything good, or positive, apart from a Higher Power. With God, we can do all things, and absolutely *anything* is possible.

We do need to depend on and trust in God. That's not using God as a crutch, that's recognizing that as finite humans we have limits and we need a Higher Power to enable us do great things.

We need God for the strength to get us through the day-to-day grind. And we need God for the breakdowns and breakthroughs.

The positivity behind our faith can create miracles.

Miracles are a gift from God.

YOU are a miracle.

Every person who is ever born is a miracle, and a gift from God. Your life is a gift from God, and how you use it can be a gift to Him.

Know yourself. Know who you are. And know who you are not. Know what you can do. And learn what is too much for you to do. Know your limits as well as your best self.

Know your value. And settle for nothing less.

Take care of yourself. Self-care is a sign of self-respect.

Be yourself. If you're a square peg it's going to feel mighty uncomfortable trying to fit into a round hole!

Comparison is the enemy. Don't try to keep up with the Jones'. You can never be as good as Betty Crocker. But you can be a kick butt baker in your own right, have your own restaurant or bakery, win awards, feed the community, and make a positive difference in the world with those things you bake with your heart, out of love.

Sharing food can be sharing your love.

And that applies to whatever feeds your soul, whatever you're passionate about, and whatever fills your heart with song. Whatever gifts you have are meant to be given and shared with others.

When you share your gift of song, people may become moved or inspired by your voice. If you have a gift of art, your art could bring beauty into someone's life who really needs it. You can use your intelligence to invent something that makes a positive difference in the world.

No one is better than you. No one is better than me. We are all important. We are all needed. We are all important. Our gifts are unique to ourselves. Our gifts are all a part of the whole. One is not more important than another. They are all important.

Our talents and gifts are priceless, and there is no one else who can do what you can do. You cannot be replaced. Your purpose cannot be given to anyone else. It is meant and intended for only you.

So, when someone else's dreams come true, don't be jealous—see that as inspiration that your own dreams can come true too! Be happy for them! Then you will share in their beautiful happiness. Then you will be a part of something bigger than yourselves.

If you long for love, and everywhere you go you seem to be encountering people who are happy and in love, then be happy for them, and realize that there is always hope for you to find love too. People fall in love and find their soul mate at any point throughout life.

If you are jealous of other people's happiness and blessings you just made yourself unhappy and cursed yourself. It's imperative on a spiritual level, to not compare yourself, or what you have, or don't have, to others. Try not to covet who they are or what they have because it will do *you* no good.

It can hurt them too.

When something good happens for you, isn't is somehow even more wonderful when people share in your joy? Then please share in other's joy as well!

Jealousy is a sign that someone else has something you want. So instead of being jealous, DO something about it!

If you envy a woman her gorgeous figure, exercise and eat better! If you envy a man his style, go out and become successful so you can buy the clothes you are jealous of. Better yet, go to a thrift store and/or an inexpensive clothing store and get the same look for less!

If you are jealous of other people's success, learn the skills you will need to learn to become successful. If you're jealous when someone else's book comes out—then write your own book!

AND buy their book and promote it—*as you would like for others to do for you.*

Contrary to the messaging of the modern day: it is not all about you. It is about them too. It's about all of us.

If you support someone else's success, you have learned an important lesson about becoming more successful yourself.

If you long for love, become the best version of yourself, so that when love finds you, you'll be ready for it. You will be a healthy person who can sustain a positive and healthy relationship.

It's important not to settle. It's important to believe you can have what you want. And in the meantime, work on becoming the best version of yourself so that when you meet the person of your dreams, or are offered the opportunity to make your dreams come true, you will be ready to receive and *act* upon it.

It's important to remain true to yourself, to find the balance between being open to people and their beliefs, and staying true to yourself, your values, and what you believe in. It's important to learn to love yourself, to stand your ground, and to be able to stand on your own two feet.

There's a balance between being open to others and losing yourself. There's a balance between being self-sufficient and having your walls up, but there may be times we have to go to either extreme to learn the lesson of striking the right balance, and finding the right people.

It is better to try and fail than to never try at all. He who dares greatly, dares to achieve great things. There is a time and place to do, and a time and place to be.

When God calls you to do something, I encourage you do it with all you've got.

I do need to warn you though. You can expect that things won't always go smoothly. Expect battles and prepare for them. Don't ever let them stop you. And celebrate all the victories along the way.

Be strong enough to stand by yourself, when necessary, smart enough to know when you need help, and courageous enough to ask for it. Be wise enough to accept the things you can't change, brave enough to change the things you can, and wise enough to know the difference.

We choose who is in our life. We can choose where we live. If we aren't happy with something in our lives, we can work to change it.

A secret to life, however, is finding joy even when things aren't perfect. Because nothing in life ever will be. Learning to enjoy the journey, makes getting to the destination a sweeter ride.

Every action we take should be motivated by love. To do so, we have to slow down a bit. Slowing down, even just a little, often prevents a lot of unnecessary mistakes. When we get frustrated, that's a sign we're going too fast, and working too hard.

Below is a poem I wrote about this very thing:

"Going with the Flow"

By Crystal Wolfe

I used to think that rushing through
Was how I was supposed to be.
But then I learned, by slowing down,
Things flowed more naturally.

I got more done, made less mistakes,
And enjoyed the work much more,
If I didn't rush through quite so much,
Work became more of a blessing, less of a chore.

I thought that life would finally start
Once I'd finished and won the race.
I thought that the faster I went,
The quicker I'd be to reaching my fate.

Doing this brought me frustration,
Until my days were full of strife.
And then I realized one fine day,
That race I was rushing through was life.

I had forgotten to live,
On the quest to my dreams.
In my need to achieve,
I'd lost the joy I used to find in simple things.

So now I take just a little more time,
To appreciate the scenery as I'm going by.
I take a few moments to say hello
And smile at the people I meet.

Because you never know,
How your dreams will unfold,
And where life can go,
If you learn to go with the flow.

Action is important. But there needs to be a give a take. If you go too fast you might make more mistakes and miss out on opportunities you just don't see because you have tunnel vision about what you think you need to do to get to where you want to be.

So, slowing down a little bit more, and appreciating your surroundings, will help you to enjoy the journey a lot more, and will actually help you to get there faster too!

Once we hit the pinnacle, there will be new dreams to discover, more lessons to uncover. New mountains to climb and new goals to reach. It is a never-ending continuum. There's always another ocean to breach, another challenge to overcome, another dream to make come true.

While it's good to have role models, like saints, friends, family, and people to look to and try to emulate for their good qualities, put your own spin on it, and don't get down on yourself if you can't be exactly like someone else. Remember: they could never be like you either.

We're all meant to be the best WE can be. Apart from everyone else, but at the same time, a part of something as a whole that is bigger than ourselves.

To be the best you, forget about being exactly like anyone else. You've got your quirks for a reason. You've got your gifts and your shortcomings for a reason to.

There's something you can do that I could never do. There's something I can do that you could never do. And I guarantee you that the world will be a better place if you figure out what that is, and you go ahead and DO IT!

Yes, you WILL fail. But fail UP. What does that mean? It means taking your failures and learning from them, so that every step you take in life is like a stepladder you are climbing towards your eventual goals, like in the illustration below.

You REALLY CAN do anything you put your mind to. If your feelings are fueling you, with gratitude in your heart, with the humility to grow, by focusing on the positive, your actions will lead to your eventual victory.

Don't doubt it. Believe it with all your heart, and mind, and body, and soul, and spirit. *Our dreams are meant to come true!!!!* Our dreams are meant to become the lives we LIVE.

Being positive makes the world a better place—for you, for me, for all of us! On our way to the finish line and the living of our dreams, being positive will make the ride that much sweeter.

You CAN do it.

But will you?

It *is* your choice.

The ball is in your court.

What action will you take?

I hope you take the shot. I hope you win.

PRACTICAL APPLICATION
For Positive Action

Prayer

Dear Lord, please help me to have right actions today. Please help me to follow you, and to follow-through on the things I said I would do. Thank you for guiding my actions to do positive and productive things.

Thank you for all I accomplish through you and by your grace. Thank you for helping me to flourish in the fruits of the spirit, so that that my actions show more of Christ, and less of me. Amen.

Meditation: Meditate 10 minutes today on what you can do TODAY to work towards your dreams. What small action steps can you take? Meditate and reflect on them. Then after you've meditated, DO THEM!

Affirmations

I am ready and willing to do God's will today.

I am equipped to do what God has called me to do. Whatever I need to learn to fulfill the callings God gave me, He will help me to learn.

My actions are not who I am; they are results of who I am.

My value is in who I am, not what I do.

I want to have positive actions.

I am ready to put action behind my words.

I do what I say I'm going to do. I have the integrity to follow-through.

I am happy to show my faith that everything will work out, by working towards my goals.

I choose to be positive in my actions today.

Declarations

I will eat curds and honey when I learn to refuse to do evil and choose the good. (Adapted from Isaiah 7:15)

Faith by itself, if it is not accompanied by action, is dead. I put my faith into action. (Adapted from James 2:17)

I am His workmanship. I was created in Christ Jesus for good works, which God prepared beforehand, that I should walk in them. (Adapted from Ephesians 2:10)

Song

"Fight Song"

By Rachel Platten

Like a small boat on the ocean
Sending big waves into motion
Like how a single word
Can make a heart open
I might only have one match
But I can make an explosion

And all those things I didn't say
Were wrecking balls inside my brain
I will scream them loud tonight
Can you hear my voice this time?

This is my fight song (Hey)
Take back my life song (Hey)
Prove I'm alright song (Hey, ha)
My power's turned on (Hey)
Starting right now, I'll be strong (Hey)
I'll play my fight song (Hey)
And I don't really care if nobody else believes (Ha)
'Cause I've still got a lot of fight left in me.

Losing friends and I'm chasing sleep
Everybody's worried about me
In too deep, say I'm in too deep (In too deep)

And it's been two years, I miss my home (I miss my home)
But there's a fire burning in my bones (In my bones)
Still believe, yeah, I still believe
You might also like

And all those things I didn't say
Wrecking balls inside my brain
I will scream them loud tonight
Can you hear my voice this time?

This is my fight song (Hey)
Take back my life song (Hey)
Prove I'm alright song (Hey, ha)
My power's turned on (Hey)
Starting right now, I'll be strong (Hey)
I'll play my fight song (Hey)
And I don't really care if nobody else believes (Ha)
'Cause I've still got a lot of fight left in me.

A lot of fight left in me.

Like a small boat on the ocean
Sending big waves into motion
Like how a single word
Can make a heart open
I might only have one match
But I can make an explosion

This is my fight song (Hey)
Take back my life song (Hey)
Prove I'm alright song (Hey)
My power's turned on (Hey)
Starting right now, I'll be strong (I'll be strong)

I'll play my fight song (Hey)
And I don't really care if nobody else believes.
'Cause I've still got a lot of fight left in me.

Yeah, I've still got a lot of fight left in me.

CHAPTER NINE
Positivity is About Endurance

The truth is that the most positive people you will meet in life have usually been through the most. The ability to keep going, to keep trying, to keep knocking on doors, until you find the door that God opens that no man can shut, is the power of persistence in action.

If you want to succeed, if you want anything good in your life, if you want to live your dreams, you are going to have to overcome a lot of tests, trials, and temptations that come your way. You are going to have to learn how to *endure* whatever comes with a good attitude, in patient, confident trust, that things will work out.

Storms pass. The sun arises every morning, come what may. What you're going through won't last forever. Remember that when the times are hard, to get you through it, and remember that in the good times too, so you remember to appreciate them.

People and circumstances will come into your life to delay you, but don't ever let anyone or anything stop you from doing what is in your heart to do, to be. This is all a part of the spiritual journey of our souls.

If you want to have a testimony, then you're going to have to pass the test. If you're going to have message, then you're going to have to learn how to clean up the mess, and learn to see those messes as blessings in disguise.

We all have to learn how to make lemonade out of lemons. We all have to learn how to endure well. To not just go on, but continue with a positive attitude, *even as* you're walking through the painful tests and trials that life brings.

Adversity is inevitable for those who are trying to achieve great things. If you want to live your dreams, the bigger the dreams, the more difficult the adversities are likely to be. We cannot avoid it.

The question is, how will we respond to it? Will we do what most people do—complain and gripe, cry, and worse of all—allow the adversity to stop us in our tracks? Will we allow these adversities to become stumbling blocks that delay or stop us, or will we use them as stepping stones, and see them as opportunities to learn and grow from?

Being positive while you're enduring painful situations is the most difficult time of all to be positive. But if you can learn to be positive during the dark times, then nothing can ever bring you down. If you can find the good in even the worst of things, then nothing and no one will ever be able to defeat you.

Then you will have learned the invaluable spiritual lesson of being grateful in every circumstance. Whether in times of plenty, or in times of lack, whatever you have can be enough with the right attitude.

You will be grateful for whatever little you have. Then, and only then, will you be rewarded with the greatest success of your life.

You will have learned the benefits of positivity even in the darkest of times.

Learning to love you yourself is about learning to take care of yourself. Doing things you enjoy will help you learn to be happy and content with your own company.

You can't pour from an empty cup. Until you learn how to fill yourself up, and be satisfied with however much you have, you will always be looking for someone else to fill that void.

We all have a Jesus-shaped hole in our hearts that only He can fill.

By connecting to a Higher Power, we are able to get through anything in life. God alone is enough to see us through the hard times. In fact, only God *can* see us through.

Depending on others will only disappoint us. No one is perfect. People will eventually die, they may change jobs and move away, or they may choose to walk away from us, forever. Depending upon God is like building your home on a rock, not the shifting sands of time, ever-changing and mutable by nature. As people can often be.

The truth is, we are never alone. Those we loved who have passed away are all around us. They are still with us. Guiding us, as our guardian angels.

There are angels surrounding us with love. And the help of God Himself is simply a breath away. He is merely waiting for you to ask for it.

Help may not be immediate. Sometimes an answer to a prayer is no, or the answer may be a long time in coming. Trusting and having confidence that your prayer was heard, that it matters, and that one way or another it will be answered, makes all the difference, as you endure tough times.

Wealth can be found in all the simple pleasures of life that are free. A bowl of fresh berries. A bright, beautiful bouquet of spring flowers after a long winter. The feel of the warm water on your skin in a happy lake in July. The first crisp, cool air of fall, and the brilliant leaves of autumn, so colorful and resplendent, they take your breath away.

You could be going through hell in your life. But you can take comfort that every day, at a certain time governed by the seasons, the sun will rise and set. You can walk through the woods every day, and notice how every day it looks a little bit different. You can learn to understand the power of how the seasons change, and every moment is in a state of flux. Yet those constant changes in life, are the very things you can always count on.

You change too. We all change. We can change to grow, and improve. We can get stuck. Or we can stop trying at all, and get worse.

We can let the pain and grief and loss we go through define us. Or we take control of our lives, and let our efforts define us. We can become a victim trapped in pain, or we can fight to be free, and learn from the experience, to become a survivor.

Most of hold sad stories in our hearts and minds, we'd rather not have happened. But when we take the time and effort to process and heal from those things, they no longer have power over us. We take our power back, and fight for everything that is in us to do, and accomplish.

The beauty of nature can be healing, and help to give you the inspiration to go on. Then, if and when you experience times when you lose it all, you still have yourself. You can stay true to yourself. And if you have God in your life, then you have everything.

You can rebuild your home after a hurricane comes and tears it down. You can start a new business, after you close the last one. You can find love again, even after you lose what you thought was the greatest love of your life.

You may lose people in your life due to death, or their choices, or yours, but the love itself will always remain, if you choose to allow those painful experiences to soften you, instead of harden you. Then your heart will love deeper each time it's broken, and the next love will be even greater.

Eventually you will be able to look back, and be grateful for the time you shared, and what it taught it you.

That's how hearts are. The strongest heart is the one who has been the most broken. The kindest heart is the one who has been the most hurt, and has experienced the most cruelty. Just as often those who are the most forgiving, are those whom much has been forgiven—and those who have forgiven much, out of love.

If you endure all of this, and more, then you will be able to face every storm that comes, and you will weather it, and you will be stronger, and better for it, in ways you cannot even imagine. Not until you go through it.

That's how you overcome it all. Not by avoiding it. Not by denying it. By facing it, and working through it. With courage, and persistence, and unending, unfailing love, for whatever it is that is your heart.

To endure, you have to allow yourself to go so deep, you feel as if you may drown in the ocean of your emotions and circumstances. If you allow yourself to go through it, you will overcome it. We need to develop the staying power that will see us through to the finish line.

It's not how we start that really matters—but how we finish.

It will not be easy. It will likely be very painful and challenging, and many times along the way you will want to quit.

Don't quit. Take a break if you need it, but don't ever quit.

It will be worth it. Because what you gain will be priceless. Whatever prize, dream, or goal you reach, isn't the true prize. The true prize are these lessons you have learned, and the character you have built.

Endurance can also be applied to our physical health. Endurance exercise training can have many positive effects on health, including your lungs, circulatory system, improved metabolism, reduction of cardiovascular risk, and reduced cardiovascular mortality.

This also can delay or prevent many diseases such as diabetes, colon and breast cancers, heart disease, and others. Some examples of physical activities that build endurance include: brisk walking or jogging, dancing, biking, swimming, climbing stairs, mountains or hills, playing sports like tennis or basketball, and doing yard work like mowing, raking, or shoveling snow.

Enduring is all about stick-to-it-ness. Determination. Devotion. Staying power.

Building Resilience Tips

- Practice acceptance
- Focus on things within your control.
- Accept change by not dwelling on the past, not worrying about the future, and practicing mindfulness in the moment.
- Prioritize relationships.
- Don't withdraw in tough times.

- Try to avoid negative people.
- Expand your social network.
- Get enough exercise.
- Practice a "mind and body" relaxation technique.

The greatest example of the power of stick-to-it-ness I learned was actually from the TV Show Grey's Anatomy. There was a character on the show that was probably my least favorite character of all of them. His name was Alex Karev.

In my opinion, he often had a bad attitude, and was the least likable and talented, intelligent, or inspiring of the characters on the show.

All the other characters on that show had something really special about them—a brilliant mind, an exceptional gift of empathy, high-level instincts, etc. that made them an excellent candidate for receiving the honor of head surgeon.

This character who I didn't like had nothing that special about him—that I could see. At first glance, he appeared to be the most ordinary. Yet HE is the one who turned out to be the interim Chief of Surgery for six months, the greatest honor any of the original group of residents could have been given.

Because all the other doctors, with all their special abilities and extraordinary gifts, failed their tests one-by-one, by giving in, and by giving up. Because this guy I didn't like stuck it through to the very end, that's why he was crowned with the highest academic achievement.

It turned out he had a special gift after all. It turned out that his gift was the most important. He persisted, he endured, and he didn't let anything stop him. It turned out, in the end, what matters most, is the resiliency to simply never GIVE UP.

This may be the greatest testimony and message of all.

Enduring is the highest, and last spiritual crown. It is the hardest spiritual gift to achieve. Those who do endure, are winners, regardless if they are recognized for it.

Talent is not enough. Intelligence won't win you the greatest success. It's how you use it that defines your character and your ability to become successful, and to stay successful and not lose it all because you lack the ability to be a good steward of all you gain.

It takes approximately 10,000 hours to develop a talent. If you're in a class all your own, it takes a great deal more.

There's a reason why 80% of the population wants to write a book and only one in a million actually do. The ability to persist against all odds is what will make you not just one in a million, but one-of-a-kind.

Tomorrow is not promised for any of us. We will all inevitably die. If you want your life to mean something significant, it's important to think about your legacy. It's important to think about what you want to leave behind.

One day, we won't be here on this earth, at least not in psychical form. Our names will be engraved on a headstone. That space between the day you were born and your death—that is your life.

What do you want your headstone to read? How do you want people to remember you? What do you want to leave behind, with a piece of your heart and soul contained in it?

If you want to live your best life, it's important to live with eternity in mind, so that when you die, whatever you did with love, will live on. Forever.

PRACTICAL APPLICATION
For Positive Endurance

Prayer

Dear Lord, please help to turn the negative, painful things I've been through, into something good, something positive that will be a benefit to others as well as to myself. Thank you for giving me the strength and resolve to stay the course, even as it gets harder as I go, in order to finish the race as winner, victorious in Christ Jesus. Help me to have a good attitude and remain stable no matter my circumstances. Amen.

Meditation: Meditate 10 minutes today on one big problem you had in your life that you were able to overcome. Think about it, visualize it, and feel how good you felt when it came to a resolution.

Now think about a current problem in your life. Don't meditate on the problem itself or spin your mind into a tizzy trying to figure out HOW to make things work out. Rather, just focus on the feeling of joy, relief, and strength you feel to have it resolved.

Affirmations

I am trusting God's timing in my life.

I don't need to understand and know everything, to trust God about everything.

I choose to wait with patience and the belief that God is going to work this situation out for the good of all involved.

I believe that I deserve good things in life.

I know that everything will work out eventually.

I know that every problem has a solution.

I can do anything I set my mind to.

I believe that every cloud has a silver lining.

I choose to stay the course and believe that I can get through anything that life throws my way.

Declarations

I am born of God. Therefore, I overcome the world. My faith makes me victorious over the world. I will face tribulation in this world, yet I have peace. I take heart, for Jesus has overcome this world. (Adapted from 1 John 5:4 and John 16:33)

I know that whatever I sow in tears, I will reap in joy—in due season. (Adapted from Psalm 126:5)

I count all trials, tests, temptations, and tribulations as joy. For the testing of my faith produces steadfastness. And when I choose to be stable and positive, in spite of what I am enduring, I will be made perfect and complete, lacking in nothing. I will stand my tests to receive the crown of life. (Adapted from James 1:2-4 and James 1:12)

Song

"You Are Loved (Don't Give Up)"
By Josh Groban

Don't give up
It's just the weight of the world
When your heart's heavy
I... I will lift it for you

Don't give up
Because you want to be heard
If silence keeps you
I... I will break it for you

Everybody wants to be understood
Well I can hear you
Everybody wants to be loved
Don't give up

Because you are loved

Don't give up
It's just the hurt that you hide
When you're lost inside
I... I will be there to find you

Don't give up
Because you want to burn bright
If darkness blinds you
I... I will shine to guide you

Everybody wants to be understood
Well I can hear you
Everybody wants to be loved
Don't give up
Because you are loved

You are loved
Don't give up
It's just the weight of the world
Don't give up
Every one needs to be heard
You are loved

About the Author

Crystal Wolfe attended college at Purdue University in Indiana and Cayuga Community College in New York. Wolfe has had articles published in newspapers and magazines across the country and is an award-winning writer.

Wolfe has put her time and resources into serving the homeless by founding her own nonprofit, The Solution to Hunger, Inc., to feed the homeless and hungry with the food excess from catering companies, schools, businesses, and restaurants—serving millions of meals to those in need. Her goal is to serve billions of meals across the nation, and perhaps one day, around the world. A portion of all book proceeds goes towards this mission.

Having often been hungry and homeless herself, she always tries to turn her difficult experiences into a lesson, a blessing, or a positive.

You can keep up-to-date with Crystal Wolfe's nonprofit work serving the homeless, upcoming novels, author talks, and other creative endeavors at her website: www.thesolutiontohunger.org

About this Book

This book is comprised of 9 chapters on 9 different principles of positivity. Each chapter discusses these principles and includes practical applications with examples, positive affirmations, declarations, meditations, prayers, illustrations, and songs to help aid you learn these principles.

This book is meant to be an encouragement and inspiration to all who read it. We can achieve and overcome anything in life...with *The 9 Principles of Positivity*.

If you enjoyed reading this book, please kindly consider taking a few minutes to write a positive review for it on Amazon and/or Goodreads!

NOVELS
By Crystal Wolfe

Non-Fiction—*Our Invisible Neighbors: Accounts, Causes, & Solutions to the Epidemic of Homelessness*

Poetry—*The Resurrected Dream: A Book of Poetry & Prose from an Awakened Soul*

Daily Devotional—*You Shall Know Them By Their Fruit: A 365 Daily Devotional for Cultivating the Fruits and Gifts of the Holy Trinity*

Self-Help—*The 9 Principles of Positivity*

The Creation Series
(Fantasy and Sci-Fi)

Volume One: *Where the Shadows Meet the Light*
Volume Two: *Within the Genesis of Time*
Volume Three: *While the Ashes Rise to Life*
Volume Four: *When the Lines of Lilith Unite*

So, Joshua called together the twelve men he
had appointed from the Israelites, one from each
tribe, and said to them, "Go over before the
ark of the LORD your God into the middle of the Jordan.
Each of you is to take up a stone on his
shoulder, according to the number of the tribes of
the Israelites, to serve as a sign among you. In the
future, when your children ask you, 'What do these
stones mean?' tell them that the flow of the Jordan
was cut off before the ark of the covenant of
the LORD. When it crossed the Jordan, the waters
of the Jordan were cut off. These stones are to be
a memorial to the people of Israel forever."

-Joshua 4:4-7, NIV

May *The 9 Principles of Positivity*, as 9 stones stacked, one upon the other, of the principles I have learned and am learning, be a part of my legacy forever. May this book me a memorial for my life that stands the test of time and inspires anyone who reads it. Amen.